Creeks & Harbours of the Solent

CALSHOT SPIT

K. Adlard Coles

Revised by David Sylvester-Bradley

Creeks & Harbours of the Solent

NEEDLES TO CHICHESTER

Ninth Edition

NAUTICAL

First Published	1933
Second Edition	1936
Reprinted	1939
Third Edition	1946
Fourth Edition	1948
Fifth Edition	1954
Sixth Edition	1959
Seventh Edition	1963
Eighth Edition	1972
Reprinted	1973
Ninth Edition	1981
Reprinted	1985

Books by K. Adlard Coles

Heavy Weather Sailing
North Biscay Pilot (with A. N. Black)
Channel Harbours & Anchorages (Solent to St. Malo)
North Brittany Harbours & Anchorages (with H. G. Hasler)
Shell Pilot to the South Coast Harbours
North Atlantic
Close Hauled (Riga to Southampton)*
In Broken Water (Solent to Baltic)*
In Finnish Waters*
Mary Anne among 10,000 Islands (Finland)*
Sailing Days*
More Sailing Days*
Sailing and Cruising*
Yacht Racing Rules Simplified*

** These titles are at present out of print*

This impression published in Great Britain by
Nautical Books
an imprint of Conway Maritime Press Ltd,
24 Bride Lane,
Fleet Street,
London EC4Y 8DR

ISBN 0 85177 366 4

Caution
While great care has been taken in the compilation of this book, it is regretted that neither the authors nor the publishers can accept responsibility for any inaccuracies or mishaps arising from the work.

Filmset and printed by BAS Printers Limited, Over Wallop, Hampshire

Contents

Preface to the Ninth Edition

This ninth edition of *Creeks and Harbours of the Solent* is again virtually a new book, so extensive have been the alterations.

The basic changes required were due to the introduction of the IALA Buoyage System A, but the task has been made more difficult by the stream of other changes which occurred while the work has been in progress. Gone are the days when this book was first written nearly 50 years ago and the harbours and their buoyage and facilities were relatively static.

For this edition Col Sylvester-Bradley has sailed to every creek and harbour, often visiting them time after time to keep his surveys and information up to date. Not only has he prepared and edited the text but he has skilfully corrected the charts by hand himself; the work entailed in these has been considerable and detailed as is shown for example in the charts of Southampton Water and Chichester Harbour.

I wish to record my thanks to Colonel David Sylvester-Bradley for his editing and thorough revision of the new edition of this book. Altogether Col Sylvester-Bradley has achieved a remarkable task for which I am personally most grateful to him.

K.A.C

ACKNOWLEDGEMENTS

Most of the charts and tidal data are based on Admiralty charts, the *Channel Pilot*, and the *Pocket Tidal Stream Atlas of the Solent and Adjacent Waters* by permission of the Controller of HM Stationery Office and the Hydrographer of the Navy. I am indebted to British Transport Docks Board, Southampton, for permission to base the chart of Southampton Water on their hydrographic surveys, and to Captain M. J. Ridge, FRICS, Hydrographer, for his help and advice. I am likewise indebted to the British Transport Docks Board, Southampton, for the surveys on which the chart of Hamble River is based, and also to the Hampshire County Council and to Captain A C.D. Leach, Harbour Master, who added information on work in progress. The chart of Lymington River is based by permission on surveys for Lymington Harbour Commissioners, with advice on work in progress from Mr F. V. Woodford, Harbour Master.

General thanks are due to the other Harbour Masters and their staffs for the assistance given in the revision necessary for this edition. In particular Mr Doe, Clerk to the Harbour Commissioners at Yarmouth; Mr Grindley, Harbour Master Beaulieu River; Mr Peter Sutton of the Esso Sailing Club at Ashlett Creek; Major S. C. Selwyn, General Manager Bembridge Harbour Improvements Co Ltd; and Captain Ian Mackay, Harbour Master and Manager of the Chichester Harbour Conservancy. Thanks also to Mr Michael Grant of Redlynch who generously processed many of the photographs without charge.

Explanation of Terms and Sailing Directions

Chart Datum. The datum of the charts in this edition is approximately LAT, which for practical purposes is the lowest predicted tide, ignoring exceptional meteorological conditions. Lowering the datum to a level to which the tide rarely falls has the pessimistic result in the Solent of showing from 1½ ft to 2 ft (0·5 to 0·6 m) less water than formerly when the chart datum was approximately at the level of MLWS (Mean Low Water Springs). Many minor creeks useful for shoal draft craft are now shown as drying out. In order to clarify the position, the tidal heights above chart datum are given at the head of each chapter and it is necessary only to add the appropriate figure to arrive at depths at MLWS and MLWN.

In the text where references are made to low water, the abbreviation CD (chart datum) is frequently added to emphasize the point that there will be more water at MLWS, which is important when calculating depths over shallows. For example, where a depth at CD on part of the Hamilton Bank off Portsmouth is given as 2 ft (0·6 m), reference to the tidal heights indicates that, with the addition of the appropriate 2 ft at MLWS, the depth will be doubled to 4 ft (1·2 m) and at MLWN there will be about 7½ ft (2·3 m), which is a very different matter.

Metrification. Charted depths and drying heights are shown on the charts in metres to the first decimal point, but as these are direct conversions from the nearest foot they remain approximate only. In the text both feet and metres are given. Distances are expressed in nautical miles and cables.

Beacons and Piles are shown either as a small round O, or symbolized as also are perches, but the latter have been omitted where the scale is too small.

Bearings. The bearings in degrees are true, but approximate bearings are expressed in magnetic points of the compass. Local variation in 1980 is about 7°W. The terms 'port' and 'starboard' refer to the side on which objects lie when the vessel is approaching from seaward.

Explanation of Terms and Sailing Directions

Abbreviations.

EC	Early Closing	Cheq	Chequered	M	Miles			V, vert	Vertical
CD	Chart Datum	Dn	Dophin	m	metres			W	White
HW	High Water	F	Fixed	Mag	magnetic			Y	Yellow
LW	Low Water	Fl	Flashing	NB	Notice Board			YC	Yacht Club
LAT	Lowest Astronomical Tide	G	Green	Or	Orange				
MHWS	Mean High Water Springs	Gp	Group	PO	Post Office				
MHWN	Mean High Water Neaps	H, horiz	Horizontal	Qk	Quick				
MLWS	Mean Low Water Springs	h, m	Hours, minutes	R	Red				
MLWN	Mean Low Water Neaps	IoW	Isle of Wight	S	Stripes				
B	Black	Iso	Isophase	s, sec	Seconds				
Bn	Beacon	L Fl	Long Flashing	SC	Sailing Club				

Sailing Directions. Whilst great care has been taken that the sailing directions and the charts in this book should be accurate, the publishers and the author cannot accept any responsibility for any errors or omissions which may have escaped notice. The author would be glad to receive any information or suggestions relating to the areas covered by this book which readers may consider would improve the book. Letters should be addressed to the author at Nautical Publishing Company, Lymington, Hampshire.

The charts in this book are based on Admiralty charts and other authorities, by kind permission. They have been enlarged, altered and amplified to embody much information obtained by the author and other yachtsmen for the areas covered. It cannot, however, be too firmly emphasized that these charts are intended to supplement, and not to supersede, ordinary navigation charts. Admiralty charts are constantly being corrected, whereas corrections in a work of this kind can be made only on the occasion of a new edition. The following Admiralty charts will be useful to yachtsmen and others cruising in Solent waters:

No. 2045 *Christchurch to Owers*
No. 2219 *Western Approaches to Solent*
No. 2040 *Solent* (western part)
No. 2793 *Cowes Harbour and River Medina*
No. 1905 *Southampton Water*
No. 2041 *Port of Southampton*
No. 394 *Solent* (eastern part including Spithead)
No. 2625 *Approaches to Portsmouth*
No. 2631 *Portsmouth Harbour*
No. 2050 *Eastern Approaches to the Solent* (Nab Tower to Spithead)
No. 3418 *Langstone and Chichester harbours*

Messrs Imray, Laurie, Norie & Wilson Ltd publish excellent yachtsmen's charts including all sections of the Solent, and there is a useful general coloured chart No. 11 of the whole area published by Messrs Edward Stanford Ltd.

With the information in this book, suitable coastal charts, corrected to date, and a good Nautical Almanac such as *Reed's Nautical Almanac*, a complete stranger should have no difficulty in keeping up to date with Solent navigation.

Chart Convention

Areas of water over 6 ft (1·8 m) in charted depth are left white, as also are marinas with varying depths. Areas of 6 ft at the new chart datum and below are blue, bounded by a dotted line. This line is drawn at the equivalent of $7\frac{1}{2}$ to 8 ft (according to the position) at MLWS, which was the approximate chart datum in previous editions. Drying areas at CD are stippled over the colour and bounded by a solid line. In some parts the edges of the channel are so steep that the 6 ft line and the drying line are so close that only the drying line can be shown on small scale.

High Water. Where there is double high water, as at Southampton at spring tides, constants on Portsmouth are given for both first and second high water. At other harbours, where there is a long stand of about 2 hours near high water, the constants are for mean HW.

Lights. Lights indicated by stars without legends or with incomplete legends represent two fixed lights arranged vertically and seen Red to port—Green to starboard, proceeding up-stream.

Channel Marking. It is a feature of many creeks described in this book that the course of the channel changes from year to year and the buoyage and leading marks are altered to suit. Thus their positions shown on the chartlets should be taken as approximate.

1 Keyhaven Lake and Anchorages

Double High Water: At Hurst, Springs −1 h 10 m, and +0 h 45 m Portsmouth. Neaps mean −0 h 5 m.
Tidal Heights above datum: (at Hurst) MHWS 9 ft (2·7 m) MLWS 1·6 ft (0·5 m) MHWN 7·6 ft (2·3 m) MLWN 4·2 ft (1·3 m).
Stream sets outside off Hurst to the westward about −1 h 10 m Portsmouth, and eastward +4 h 45 m.
Depths above datum: Bar practically dries out. Over 2 fathoms (3·6 m) off the Camber, gradually decreasing to 5 ft (1·5 m) off Mount Lake and to a few inches (0·2 m) off the quay.
Yacht Clubs: Keyhaven Yacht Club, Hurst Castle Sailing Club.

Keyhaven, on the mainland shore, is the most westerly of the Solent creeks. It lies behind Hurst Castle, which dominates the narrows of the Needles Channel. Before being taken to the scaffold, King Charles I was imprisoned here in a grim dungeon in the old round castle, but the rest of the building dates only from Victorian times and consists of flat masonry relieved by the red low and the white high lighthouses.

From Hurst to the mainland there is a mile of narrow, high beach which provides a natural breakwater against the prevailing winds to protect the entrance and 'Lake', or creek, which winds its way through the marram grass-covered marshes to Keyhaven. This peaceful harbour has changed little, apart from the greatly increased membership of the clubs and the demand for every possible mooring site. It is a friendly centre for small cruising yachts and keen sailors.

North Channel and Shingles

When sailing to the Solent from the west to Keyhaven, the North Channel may be better than the Needles Channel and is considered safer in gales. Coming from the westward a yacht should be steered with Hurst High Light bearing 097° until the North Head G buoy (*Gp Fl (3) G 10s*) is sighted. Then steer to leave it to starboard and round into the channel running SE parallel with Hurst Beach. This gives about 10 ft (3·0 m) at CD.

If a leading line is desired it is the right extreme of Golden Hill Fort 118° in line with Brambles Chine. The latter is on the middle of the coast of Colwell Bay and the fort (with flagstaff) is at the summit of the hill ½ mile inland.

A useful lead in good weather, if wishing to take the short cut across the neck of the Shingle Bank between the North Head and the main part of the bank, is to keep Hurst Castle open its own width to the *left* of Sconce Point. This gives 10 ft (3·0 m) at low water *neap* tides, or 6½ ft (2·0 m) at MLWS but should be regarded with caution, as the Shingle Banks are apt to shoal or shift and the channel is narrow. The lead, incidentally, is on the direct course from Hurst to Poole Bar buoy.

1.1. Hurst Castle from the South. 'The Trap' extends approximately three quarters of a cable south from the round fort, almost directly towards the camera.

Approach, Entrance and Channel

Approaching Hurst from the westward avoid 'The Trap', a shingle bank extending three-quarters of a cable S(Mag) from the Round Fort with little water over it at chart datum. It is in the form of a gravel projection from the beach, steep on each side. Once round the 'Trap' and Hurst Point it is possible to sail NE close inshore as far as the High Lighthouse and the old pier. Here the tidal streams vary and there is an eddy close inshore. Northward of the pier the shore is more shelving and shallow water extends seawards for a considerable distance off the cottages, and develops into a wide bar across the entrance to the river. The approach is sheltered from SW through west to north, but exposed to the east, and strangers should not attempt entry in strong winds from this direction.

Make good a position about 3 cables NE of Hurst High Light when the leading marks will be seen. These consist of a front (lower) post, and a rear (higher) post both of which carry crosses (see photograph on page 16). They are situated well up on the flats. Since the 8th Edition, they have been re-newed, but the perches in the river have largely decayed and the channel is now marked by buoys and moorings. Bring the marks into line and steer on their transit. A degree of accuracy is now recommended as a shoal is building up N of the transit. The bar nearly dries out at chart datum but about 2 ft (0·6 m) can be expected at MLWS and there is said to be over 4 ft (1·2 m) at MLWN

The feature of the entry to the river is the North Point of the sand and shingle promontory extending in a NNW direction for nearly ½ mile from Hurst Point, not to be

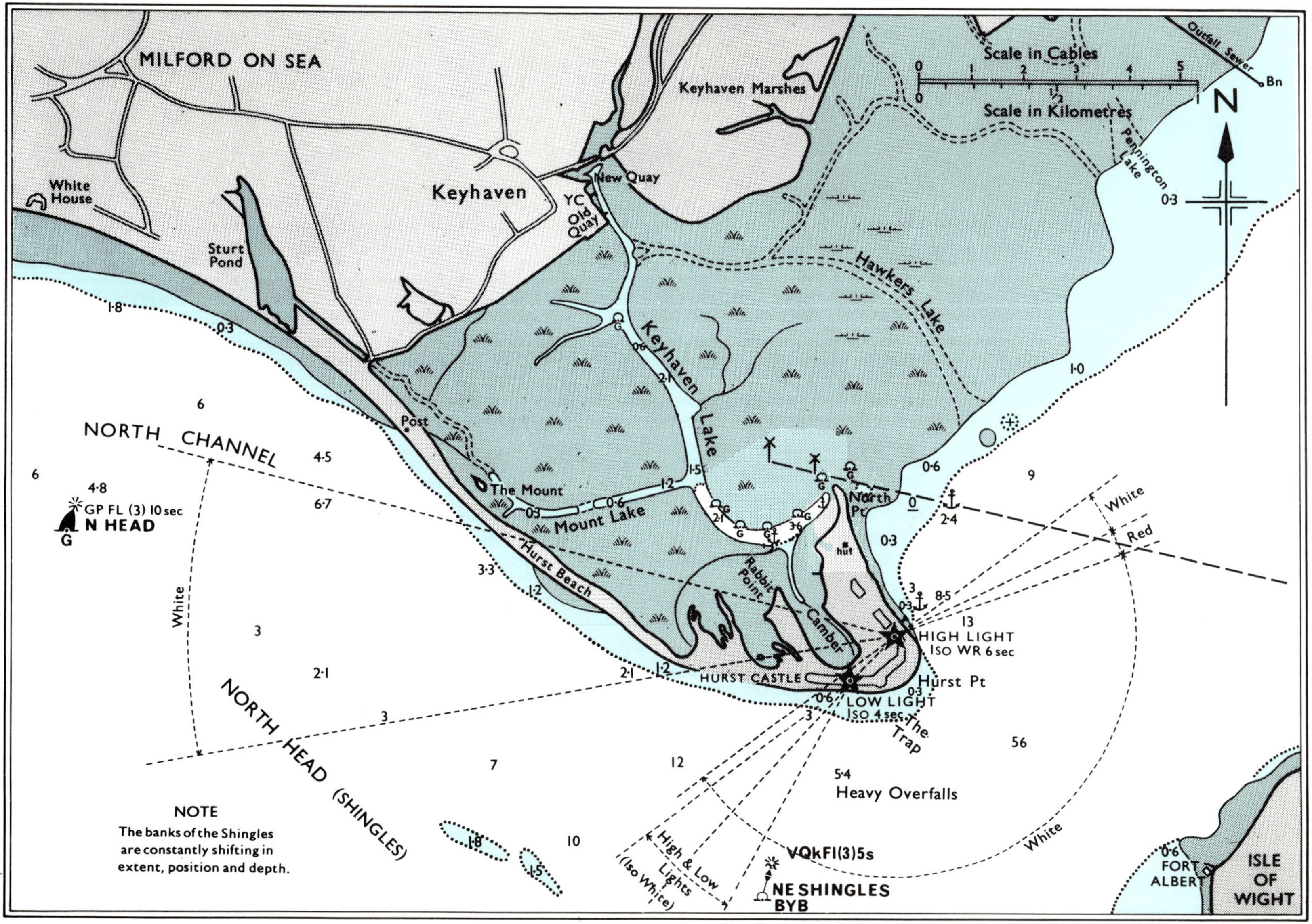

Keyhaven Lake: Soundings in metres. Add 0·5 m (1·6 ft) at MLWS, 1·3 m (4·2 ft) at MLWN. Based on British Admiralty Chart No. 2219, with the permission of HM Stationery Office and of the Hydrographer of the Navy.

1.2. Hurst castle and the entrance to Keyhaven River from the air looking south. *Photo: Brian Manby.*

confused with the long Hurst Beach to Milford-on-Sea. For some years North Point has been moving eastward and there now is a constriction of the current between the point and the mud bank. As a result the channel round North Point is well scoured, the deep water being close in; this action seems to be throwing up a shoal a little farther north. Continue on the transit of the leading marks until the apex of North Point comes abeam leaving a green buoy to starboard. A second green buoy lies close ahead. Alter course to port well before reaching this buoy and steer to pass about 30 ft (9 m) off the extremity of North Point leaving a second green buoy to starboard. This is the narrowest part of the channel and there is only about 50 ft (15 m) between the point and the buoy. Follow the shingle point round (once round it the channel quickly deepens to over 2 fathoms (3·6 m)) leaving another green buoy to starboard. The channel then leads about WSW and the stream, which may be strong off the point, weakens.

1.3. Approaching North Point which can be seen on the left.

1.4. The leading marks at the entrance to Keyhaven River 1980

Approaching from the eastward it is merely necessary to keep in sufficient depth of water, steering for the High Light and pier, until on the transit of the leading marks, when proceed as before. The stream along the Hampshire coast is much weaker inshore where it pays to cheat a foul tide, but give the sewer outfall beacons a berth of $\frac{1}{4}$ mile at low water, and note that there is an obstruction and shoal SE of the entrance to Hawker's Lake.

After entering Keyhaven Lake at North Point a misleadingly wide expanse of water will be seen ahead if it is near high water, as shown in the aerial photograph. The lake on the port hand is the Camber, but at low tide most of this dries out leaving only a short creek leading to a dilapidated private landing stage and a longer creek beyond it, 2 ft (0·6 m) at LW Neaps, which winds its way through the mud to a quay near Hurst Castle. Likewise there will be a camber seen ahead north of Rabbit Point, leading westerly to Hurst beach, but this also dries out, although a few light draft yachts are moored near its entrance.

The picture at low water would be very different as the navigable river is then comparatively narrow. It bends round a semi-circle of gently sloping mud bank (much of which is covered at HW) from SW through west and NW almost to north. The bend in the channel is well marked by three more green buoys on the starboard side. One has now passed six green buoys and there is but one more, at the approach to the upper or short reach. The channel is at least 7 ft (2·1 m) deep as far as Mount Lake, which branches off to the westward towards Hurst Beach. Above Mount Lake the river narrows and the depth falls to 5 ft and 4 ft (1·5 m and 1·2 m) for 2 cables and then to 3 ft (0·9 m) before the last reach, which practically dries out. The line of moorings in the centre of the river shows the direction of the channel very clearly but, if the wind is blowing the yachts broadside across the fairway, steer across their bows rather than under their sterns which may be close to the mud. In the upper reach there are two lines of small craft and the best water is between them close to the port hand line leaving a green buoy to starboard, although from its position one would expect it to be port hand. When the old quay is abeam keep to port close to the stakes which remain from an ancient quay.

Mount Lake has 4 ft (1·2 m) at CD for over a cable from its entrance and is navigable for most of its length with sufficient rise of tide, but strangers may not find the best water as in the channel this is only about 40 ft (12 m) wide.

Lights: Keyhaven Lake has no lights, but entrance is possible if it is not too dark to identify North Point and craft moored in the river.

Moorings, Anchorage and Facilities

Moorings are laid almost everywhere from the Camber to Keyhaven and in Mount Lake. Even in Hawker's Lake there are moorings for shallow draft yachts which can dry out. Moorings should not be picked up without local advice as the owners usually return in the evenings. The only position left for anchoring is just within the entrance WSW of North Point, where the water is deep but there is room only for a few yachts. The position can be uncomfortable in strong SW winds and it is best to moor with two anchors which should be buoyed. Telegraph cables cross the river twice at the bend between the Camber and Mount Lake and are also laid on the river bed farther up, where if anchoring temporarily in an emergency be sure to use a really strong tripping line.

There is anchorage outside off the mud flats in NW winds but the popular one is under the lee of the shingle bank between the old pier near the High Light and the cottages just north of it, where the water begins to shoal and anchorage is necessarily farther out. The anchorage is sheltered from SW, W and NW winds but suffers from the swell of passing ships. It is used principally in day time when as many as twenty or more yachts bring up on a summer afternoon, and use dinghies to land on the shingle or to proceed up the river to Keyhaven. During gales the anchorage is uncomfortable owing to tidal eddies but it provides tolerable shelter in good holding ground and may be useful if arriving at night when the tide is turning foul in the Solent.

At Keyhaven there is a poor public landing on steps at the end of the old quay and a new quay beyond the yacht clubs with dinghy landing at the hard adjacent to it. The River Warden (Mr. M. Woods) has a temporary (1980) office on the promontory about ½ cable north of the old quay and near The Keyhaven Yacht Club (with it's private dinghy pontoon) and the Hurst Castle Sailing Club. Close to the clubs there is the yacht yard of the West Solent Boat Builders who undertake laying-up and repairs and provide fuel and water for yachts. At the hard, where there is 6 ft (1·8 m) at HW Springs, yachts can be scrubbed, and there is a launching site for dinghies, though it is often congested in the season, particularly at week-ends. Behind the Keyhaven Yacht Club there is a car park and the Gun Inn is just across the road. There is a small general stores and PO (EC Thursday)

1.5. Keyhaven Y.C. and dinghy pontoon. To the right is the new quay and between the two is the dinghy hard.

about a cable to the right and a private hotel where meals may be had if ordered in advance. Buses very occasionally run to Milford-on-Sea, a mile distant, where there are the usual facilities of a small town (EC Wednesday). In summer there are motor launches from the quay to Hurst Castle, which is maintained by the Ministry of Works and is open to the public.

Nearby Anchorages

Yarmouth Roads is the nearest anchorage to Hurst Road—see Yarmouth—but there are two interesting ones in the Needles Channel. The nearest is Totland Bay (distance only 1½ miles from Hurst) which is sheltered in southerly and easterly winds. Anchor according to draft off the pier outside local moorings but inside the moorings of the pilot, in from 5 ft to 1 ft (1·5 m to 0·3 m) CD. The *FR* light at the pier head enables the anchorage to be used at night under suitable conditions. Hotel near pier and there are shops at Totland.

Alum Bay, over a mile farther towards the Needles, is famous for its multi-coloured cliffs at the foot of which there are sands suitable for children. There is a cliff path leading to large motor coach and car parks, the Royal Needles Hotel (non-residential but with snack bar and restaurant open in summer) and a café. Nowadays there may be many yachts in the bay on a summer's day. The anchorage is good in southerly and easterly winds, though during gales squalls come down from the cliffs above. If sheltering in a southerly gale be prepared to leave quickly in the event of the wind veering later towards NW, as this may put the yacht on a lee shore. The anchorage is little used at night but the Shingles buoys are an aid to navigation. The best position is off the ruins of the pier, of which only one pile and an inner pair remain standing. Less than a cable to the northward of the approach is the Five Finger Rock 2 ft (0·6 m) CD, and to the southward the Long Rock, dries 4 ft (1·2 m), and a detached rock east of it, half way to the shore. Both Five Finger and Long Rock can be avoided by keeping Warden Fort open of Hatherwood Point until what is left of the ruined pier bears East (mag), then sail in to the required depth of water—see chart. Owners familiar with Alum Bay may pass between the ledges off Hatherwood Point and Five Finger Rock.

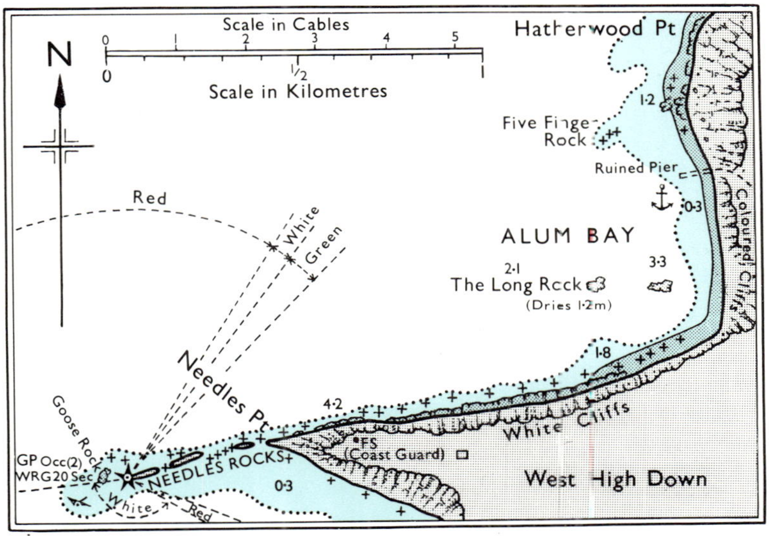

Alum Bay: Based on British Admiralty Chart No. 2219, with the permission of HM Stationery Office and the Hydrographer of the Navy.

2 Yarmouth Harbour

Double High Water: Springs − 1 h 5 m and + 0 h 50 m. Portsmouth. Neaps mean + 0 h 5 m.
Tidal Heights above datum: MHWS 10·1 ft (3·1 m) MLWS 1·9 ft (0·6 m) MHWN 8·3 ft (2·5 m) MLWN 4·6 ft (1·4 m).
Stream sets outside strongly to the westward − 1 h 15 m Portsmouth and to the eastward + 4 h 50 m.
Depths above datum: 7 ft (2·1 m) in the approach channel and about 6 ft (1·8 m) in the harbour itself.
Yacht Clubs: Royal Solent Yacht Club, Yarmouth Sailing Club.

Yarmouth is undoubtedly the most popular of the Solent harbours for visiting yachts, being at a convenient distance from most centres in the Solent and providing good deep water berths. The harbour is very well run for yachtsmen and provides the best port of departure if bound west or to France.

The town itself has a mellow charm and the castle at the harbour entrance lends a mediaeval appearance as viewed from the sea.

In the Middle Ages Yarmouth and its harbour provided the first objective for attack by any French squadrons entering the Solent. It was not until the castle was built for its defence in 1537 that the town really began to prosper and grow. This massive building still remains in good condition and is preserved as an ancient monument. Behind the castle stands what was once the house of the Governor of the Island, where Charles II made a short stay while on a visit to Hurst. It is now the George Hotel, much frequented by yachtsmen.

At high water a dinghy can proceed up the River Yar and along the winding creek nearly to Freshwater. The surrounding woods, the reeds and pools backed by hills make this a pleasant trip. There are coastal walks from Yarmouth in the direction of the Needles and eastwards to Newtown. The harbour is a good place for children as there are always people about, and there is bathing from the beach to the westward.

The Approach and Entrance

Approaching from the west there are two things to consider. In deep water by the Black Rock buoy some three-quarters of a mile to the west of the entrance there is Fiddler's Race, a genuine small scale race, that can be dangerous for dinghies and unpleasant for yachts of small size; and farther inshore lies the rock itself which dries 2 ft (0·6 m) at low tide. Small craft can pass inside the rock, thus avoiding the race, by keeping the end of the pier, a cable east of Sconce Point, in line with Hurst Castle; this course is said to allow 2 ft (0·6 m) at MLWS, but almost dries out at chart datum.

The approach from the east is easy, and it is only necessary to make allowance for the strong tidal streams. By keeping on a course a little outside the end of the pier there is

2.1. Aerial photograph of Yarmouth Harbour looking north-east. *Photo: Brian Manby.*

ample water for any yacht. Small craft can keep farther inshore to cheat the tide, except at low water, when there is very little depth inside the pier end of the east side.

Make a position about $\frac{1}{4}$ cable west of the end of Yarmouth Pier and bring the leading marks (black and white diamonds on posts set behind the quay) into line at 187°. Steer on or close to this transit, but avoid being set too far eastward of it by wind or tide or when tacking. The channel narrows as the entrance is approached but carries 7 ft (2·1 m) as far as the ferry jetty and 6 ft (1·8 m) beyond it. Course should be altered to leave the jetty and ramp to port.

When the ferry ramp comes abeam to port, the main channel turns to the west parallel with the inside of the breakwater, leaving the A line of mooring piles for larger yachts to starboard and the B line to port. In addition there are three lines of mooring piles for smaller yachts with narrow fairways between them. Incoming yachts should have warps and fenders ready and are usually hailed from a boat by the Harbour Master giving

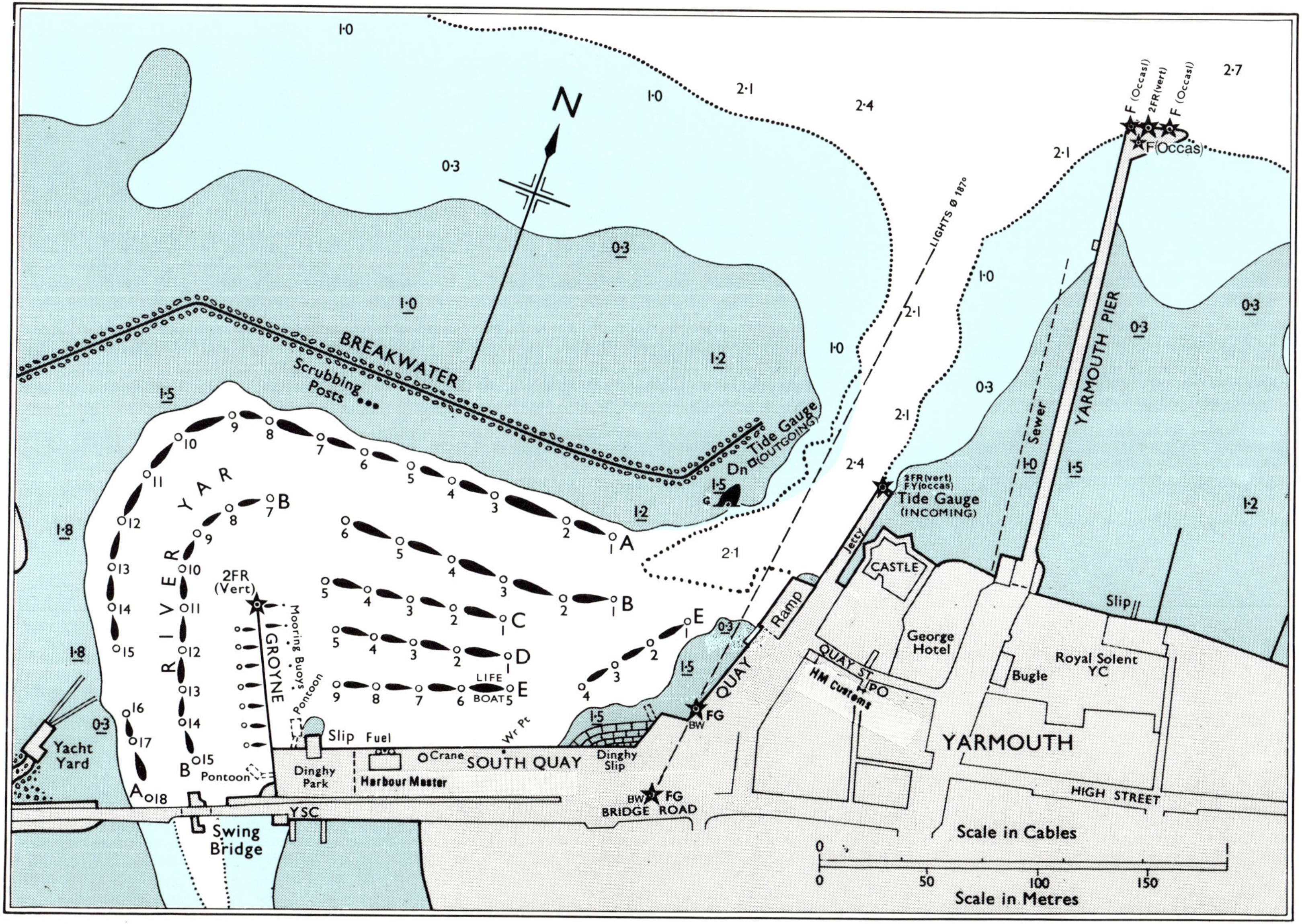

Yarmouth Harbour: Soundings in metres. Add 0·6 m (1·9 ft) at MLWS, 1·4 m (4·6 ft) at MLWN. Based on British Admiralty Chart No. 2040, with the permission of HM Stationery Office and of the Hydrographer of the Navy.

2.2. Approaching the entrance showing the ferry slip and pier in the centre and the dolphin on the starboard side of the entrance channel.

berthing instructions. If the Harbour Master or his Deputy is not immediately available it is best to berth temporarily and await directions, as anchoring is prohibited.

Within the harbour there is not a great range of tide, only about 8 ft (2·4 m) on ordinary spring tides, but the stream can be quite strong, especially on the ebb. There is then little room for tacking in the narrow fairway, especially if other craft or dinghies are under way, unless the yacht is small or very handy. Auxiliary power is usually used. Motor yachts must proceed at reduced speed. Depths vary within the harbour which tends to silt but is dredged area by area during the winter. In 1970, for example, there was 8 ft (2·4 m) along the South Quay but less between A and B lines, so it is best to regard the whole harbour as about 6 ft (1·8 m). There are three tide gauges, one on the pier, another on the ferry jetty for incoming vessels, and one facing south on the dolphin opposite for vessels leaving the harbour.

Entry Prohibited: When the harbour is full a red flag is hoisted at a flagpole at the seaward end of the ferry jetty. Yarmouth is so popular that the harbour is usually full by 5 pm on Saturdays in summer although, in the event of a yacht leaving, the Harbour Master may authorize a small yacht to enter and occupy the vacant berth.

Lights: There are two fixed green lights on the leading marks. The end of the pier outside the harbour is marked by two fixed red lights and in fog two white lights are shown as well. The end of the ferry jetty is marked by two fixed red lights and in fog a fixed yellow light. At the far end of the quay there is a fixed white light facing the harbour, showing red towards the quay itself. There are also two vertical red lights on the end of the groyne at the west end of the harbour and a flood-lit pontoon providing the Pilot Boat berth.

2.3. View of breakwater and harbour from the castle. The widest fairway for an incoming yacht lies between the outer lines of piles A. and B. Smaller yachts may be directed along the left arrow to lines C, D, or E.

Moorings, Anchorages and Facilities

The harbour comes under the authority of the Yarmouth Harbour Commissioners, whose powers are widened under an Act of Parliament to include the approach, the pier and water adjacent to it, and also the River Yar above the bridge. The speed limit is 4 knots.

Yarmouth is a natural yacht harbour but the dredging in 1958, and the South Quay which followed, enclosed some 70 acres accommodating about 300 yachts, and more at times. The development was an example of enterprise long before the creation of any marinas in this country. Dredging and improvements have continued and the harbour is a model for good relations between the controlling authority and the yachtsmen using it. Harbour dues are reasonable and special annual terms can be arranged.

Yachts berth fore and aft to the piles of which there are five lines, A, B, C, D and E and the piles on each line are numbered from the entrance. The berth between No 5 and 6 E piles is allotted to the lifeboat. Care must be taken always to moor to the piles and not to other yachts, apart from breast ropes or temporarily on arrival or departure. At the west end of the harbour there are also berths for a few small craft to moor bows to piles and sterns to the groyne.

When the harbour is full, anchorage may be found outside, large yachts usually bringing up to the west of the pierhead clear of the entrance channel and to the south of the big ship moorings, and smaller ones farther inshore according to their draft and the tidal conditions. This anchorage is reasonable in offshore winds or in settled weather, but the streams are strong so it is best to anchor as close inshore as safety permits. The anchorage is exposed to all northerly winds and it is said that in the gale of 1876 a ketch of 6 ft (1·8 m) draft, anchored in the roads, was swept by huge seas right over the breakwater, which presumably was then lower than it is today. In northerly gales and on a big spring tide even the harbour itself can be uncomfortable near high water.

On the east side of the pier there are private moorings for small craft but room can usually be found for yachts of light draft to anchor in settled weather. This position gets some protection by the pier from the prevailing winds and is convenient for the club and the town. Whether anchoring to the west or east of the pier there is often a roll, even if only from passing ships.

If a prolonged stay at Yarmouth is intended in a small yacht, it is worth consulting the Harbour Master (Mr C. Attrill, whose office is on the South Quay, Tel: Yarmouth 760300) about passing through the swing bridge into the River Yar. He can advise about moorings or anchorage, as there is not so much room as there used to be, and he also arranges the time at which the bridge, which is electrically controlled, can be opened. There is a strong stream at times.

Landing in Yarmouth Harbour is easy as there are several slips and pontoons. There is a crane, fuel pumps, water, a marine engineer's workshop (where batteries can be

2.4. Dinghy pontoon and small yacht berths at the groyne at the west end of the harbour.

charged), slipway and dinghy compound at the South Quay. This extends the whole length of the bridge road between the training groyne and the town. Yachts may go alongside for petrol, water, etc. At the time of writing the depth is 8 ft (2·4 m) but it is safer to take it as 6 ft (1·8 m). There are two scrubbing berths on piles near the breakwater for yachts up to 6 ft (1·8 m) draft on application to the Harbour Master, and scrubbing berths at the quay, except during the holiday period or busy week-ends when the space is required for landing purposes.

The town of Yarmouth itself is well adapted to the needs of yachtsmen. The Royal Solent YC is a leading and hospitable yacht club and the Yarmouth SC has been re-established, two hotels (the George and the Bugle), the Wheatsheaf restaurant and other inns and small restaurants. Customs formalities are quick as their office (Quay Street) is open from 6 am to 10 pm in summer months. J. Cook's supply yacht chandlery, hardware, petrol, paraffin and an amazing variety of yacht requirements. The PO is in Quay St, next to Holding's booksellers, stationers and newsagents (including Sunday papers), and there are small shops of all kinds, EC Wednesday. There are three yacht yards: Harold Hayles (Yarmouth IW) Ltd, just west of the bridge, and above the bridge Theo Smith & Son, and the River Yar Boat Yard which lays up many yachts. Yacht brokers are Harold Hayles Ltd, and West Solent Yacht Agencies Ltd. Launching sites from dinghy slips at the quays or from the ferry slip by arrangement with Harbour Master. Car park adjacent. The lifeboat is famous for her work in the Needles Channel and south of the Island. Frequent ferries run to Lymington and in the summer there are occasional excursion steamers to Bournemouth and elsewhere. Sand Hard Ferries provide a useful local service from the stops to the bathing beach and to yachts. There are good bus connections.

3 Lymington River

Double High Water: Springs −0 h 55 m and +0 h 45 m Portsmouth; Neaps mean +0 h 5 m.
Tidal Heights above datum: MHWS 10 ft (3·0 m) MLWS 1·6 ft (0·45 m) MHWN 8·4 ft (2·6 m) MLWN 4·4 ft (1·3 m).
Stream sets to the westward off Lymington Spit about −1 h 15 m Portsmouth, and eastward +4 h 50 m.
Depths: There is a minimum depth of 6 ft (1·8 m) in mid-channel from the river entrance to the pier railway station and Berthon Boat Co Ltd, gradually shoaling towards the channel margins. From the Berthon to the Town Quay and bridge there is a least depth of 3½ ft (1·1 m). The width of the channel above Harper's Post is restored by dredging from time to time.
Yacht Clubs: Royal Lymington Yacht Club, Lymington Town Sailing Club.

The channel winds its way through marshes to Lymington, the old world town whose history from far into the past has been associated with ships and the sea. At one time it was an important local centre of salt and iron-smelting industries, the ironstone being quarried at Hengistbury and brought to Lymington by sea in barges and beaten out by great hammers worked by water wheel from the 'hammer ponds', of which Sowley is one. 'Jack in the Basket', the beacon with a barrel top in the approach to Lymington, used to be taken as a point of departure for ships, and it was from here that HMS *Pandora* sailed in 1790 to search the Pacific for the mutineers from the *Bounty*.

Today the river is little used for commercial purposes other than by the car ferries to Yarmouth, but it has grown to be an important yachting centre with two of the leading marinas in the Solent and many river moorings. The river is deep enough for most yachts except very deep draft craft at extreme LW springs and the yachting facilities are excellent. The town itself has grown but it retains its character and much of its old-world charm.

The Approach, Entrance and River

When entering the river the best water will be found by leaving Jack in the Basket about 150 ft to port to clear Cross Boom (next port hand pile) by approximately 120 ft to port. Thereafter the river is well marked by red piles with can type topmarks on the port hand and by green piles with green triangular topmarks to starboard. The deepest part of the fairway in cross-section is about in the middle third as the channel tends to shoal toward the sides. The beacons should be given a wide berth as many of them are on the mud or in very shallow water. The line of yachts on moorings near the mud on the west side of the river provide an additional aid to pilotage. The bank on the east side at the end of the first Long Reach has been dredged away to make the channel 250 ft (76 m) wide, providing room for the ferries on half-hourly service to pass each other at low water. The alterations are shown on the accompanying chart. Two leading posts, with red and white horizontal stripes, are erected on the flats to the south of Seymore's Post to provide a transit for the outgoing ferries and another pair, with black and white horizontal

3.1. The entrance from the south-east showing from right to left in the foreground the R. Lymington Y.C. starting platform, the yellow diamond post on the starting line, and river post No. 1, all of which have to be left to starboard.

stripes, on the flats on the east side of the river south of the Cage Boom for the incoming ferry transit.

The car ferries are the only features disconcerting to the stranger. These are handled with care but are big for the river and should not be passed too closely, especially by dinghies, owing to the suction they cause in the restricted water. The ferries have right of way and can be quite a problem at low water if several yachts are in the vicinity at the same time.

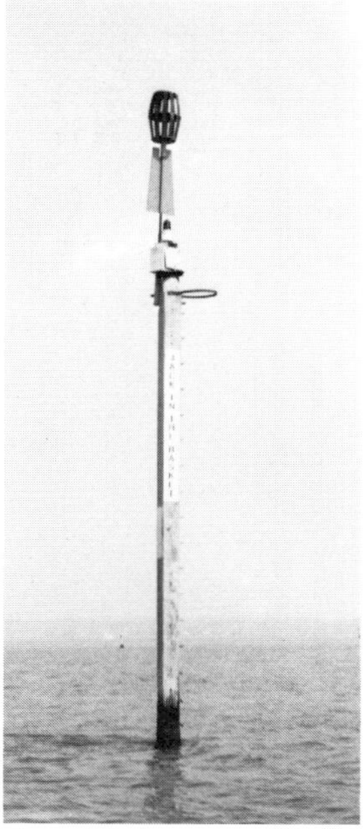

3.2. Jack-in-the-Basket at the mouth of the river on the west side.

3.3. Harper's Post at the entrance to the Lymington Yacht Haven.

Horn Reach, which is the last reach up to the Pier railway station, is the narrowest. Harper's Post, at the entrance to the Lymington Yacht Haven, is the first port hand mark in this reach, which leads past the landing slip, the Bath Road public pontoon and the Royal Lymington Yacht Club's pontoon off which local racing classes are moored. Beyond these, also on the port hand, lies the Lymington Marina, and the main channel leads between the marina and the Pier ferry terminal and station. It then bends round the end of the marina, leaving a short line of mooring piles (some painted red) to port and a longer line of black piles to starboard, and turns to the west towards the Berthon Boat Co Ltd, leaving a wide expanse of mud on the starboard hand. This part of the channel above the ferry terminal is slightly narrower due principally to the craft moored on piles on either side. Subject to silting it carries 6 ft (1·8 m) as far as the yacht yard, and $3\frac{1}{2}$ ft (0·9 m) beyond it. Finally after passing the yacht yard there is a short reach up to the railway bridge, leaving the Town Quay on the port side.

Lights: There are two fixed red lights near the yacht club which lead up the first reach at 320° up to Seymore's Post. The river is marked on the port side by five *Fl R* lights and on the starboard hand by seven *Fl G* during the hours of darkness throughout the year.

3·4. The public pontoon. The R. Lymington Y.C. and the club pontoon and the reach past Lymington Marina up to the pier ferry terminal.

Moorings, Anchorage and Facilities

Anchorage is prohibited in the river, which is fully occupied by moorings controlled by the Harbour Commissioners and mostly rented annually, but anchorage can be found outside off the mud flats in offshore winds. The principal centre in the river is the marina of the Berthon Boat Company which is situated on the west side of the river and has 240 berths. Most of the berths are rented in advance for the season but visitors can usually be temporarily accommodated, preferably by telephoning in advance. There is also the Lymington Yacht Haven marina in Harper's Lake which has 430 berths.

The Harbour Master (Mr. F. V. Woodford (Tel: Lymington 72014) will advise on the

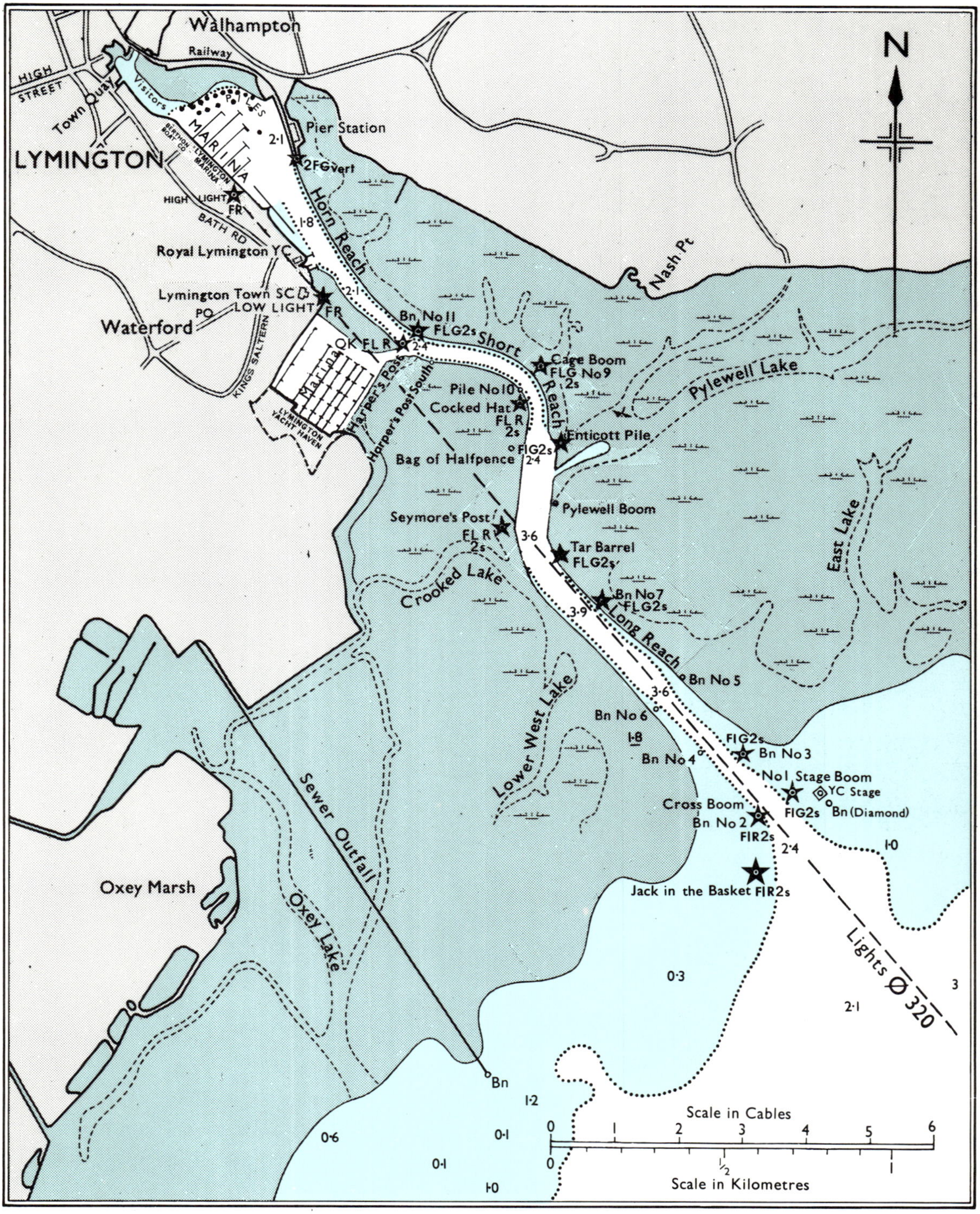

Lymington River: Soundings in metres. Add 0·5 m (1·6 ft) at MLWS, 1·3 m (4·4 ft) at MLWN. Based on surveys by permission of Lymington Harbour Commissioners. Approaches based on British Admiralty Chart No. 2040, with the permission of HM Stationery Office and of the Hydrographer of the Navy.

3·5. The marina and Berthon Boat Co. Ltd., showing the trend of the river towards the Town Quay. *Photo: Brian Manby.*

use of the Town Quay and moorings in the river. His office is near to the R Lymington YC. An area has been dredged on the opposite side of the river to the Town Quay where moorings with white buoys have been laid for visiting yachts, with a depth of about 5 ft (1·4 m) which is likely to be dredged to 7 ft (1·8 to 2·1 m) MLWS. At the Custom's House Quay (just downstream of the Town Quay) there are pontoons where yachts can bring up six abreast with about 2 ft (0·2 m) at the inmost berth and 4½ ft (1·4 m) three berths out at MLWS. Altogether there are now berths for about 100 visiting yachts, apart from the marinas. Yachts up to 6 ft (1·8 m) draft may be scrubbed at the Town Slip, but the time must be arranged with the Harbour Master. Car park, water and public lavatories are adjacent and also the Ship Hotel and restaurant, two chandlers and nearby in Quay Hill a good shop for yachting clothes and oilskins.

The largest yacht yard is the Berthon Boat Co Ltd, just north of their marina, which

3.6. The upper harbour showing in the centre background the ferry pier and marina, nearer the foreground in the centre the visitors moorings and on the right the public pontoons against the quay wall. The picture faces S.E.

has craftsmen for all kinds of repairs and yacht building, including ocean racers and has a chandlery and garage. The customs office, with 24 hours service, is situated with the Harbour Master in a three storey building between R Lym YC and the Lym Town SC. The Lymington Yacht Haven at Waterford has an extensive chandlery. Mr Bill Smith has moved his yacht repairing, laying up and boat transport facilities to the yard by the station in Mill Lane. J. C. Rogers in Station Yard build Contessas and other fibreglass designs. Other builders are Aquaboats and Pegasus Marine in Mill Lane nearby. Laurent Giles and Partners, the yacht designers and agents, are in Quay Hill, while Hoods, sailmakers, and Brookes & Gatehouse, electronic instrument makers, are close to the Berthon Boat Co Ltd. In addition there are several smaller firms supplying yachting requirements such as sails, clothing and chandlery, as well as the Nautical Publishing Company in Station Street.

The R Lymington YC and the Lymington Town SC are at Waterford where there are car parks adjacent to the clubs and a small general stores with an off licence (EC Thursday mornings, but open Sundays) which also sells newspapers. A Sub-Post Office (also grocers, EC Mondays) is in Westfield Road 200 yards west of Bath Road.

Water can be had at the marina pontoons, at the Town Quay and the Bath Road public pontoon and at yacht yards. Fuel at the Marina pontoons and yacht yards. Launching sites at public slipway adjacent to yacht clubs or at the Town Quay.

The main shopping centre is in the High Street, which despite the addition of a few multiple shops has changed little over the centuries, and leads up the hill from Quay Street to St Thomas' church. Here will be found banks and good individual shops of

Visitors moorings Public pontoons and Quay

every description, including a leading bookshop and a toy shop so intriguing that children should be kept away from its temptation. EC Wednesday. There are also hotels: Angel, Stanwell House and others; restaurants and garages and good travel agents. Communications are excellent: from pier and town stations to Brockenhurst linking up with fast electric trains (Waterloo, Southampton, Bournemouth and Weymouth), buses to all parts and frequent car ferries to Yarmouth, IOW. The New Forest, with its lovely countryside is within easy reach.

4 Newtown River

Double High Water: Springs about −1 h 0 m and +0 h 50 m Portsmouth; Neaps mean −0 h 5 m.
Tidal Heights above datum at Solent Banks: MHWS 11·2 ft (3·4 m) MLWS 1·6 ft (0·5 m) MHWN 9·2 ft (2·8 m) MLWN 4·8 ft (1·5 m).
Stream sets outside to the westward −1 h 15 m Portsmouth, and to the eastward +4 h 45 m.
Depths: About 3 ft (0·9 m) on the bar; 5 ft (1·5 m) to 11 ft (3·3 m) in channel as far as Fishhouse Pt 4 ft (1·2 m) with deeper pools within, falling to 3 ft (0·9 m) at junction with Causeway Lake and shallow beyond.

There must be few yachtsmen who, after visiting Newtown for the first time, have not returned to it again year after year. The snug anchorage, the creeks winding silently through the marshes and the unspoilt countryside, combine to give the place a character of its own. Perhaps the finger-prints of history linger on in some distant way to the present time.

Newtown, under its original name of Francheville, was once the capital of the Isle of Wight and a flourishing seaport. In 1377 the town was sacked and burnt by the French. When partially rebuilt, the name was changed to Newtown, but it was too vulnerable to attack from the sea for its former prosperity to be regained. However, from 1585 to 1832 it returned two members of Parliament, which included John Churchill, later Duke of Marlborough. The old town hall has been skilfully restored and maintained in perfect repair by the National Trust, and is well worth visiting. There are still lanes and cuttings through the trees that once were busy streets some 600 years ago.

The village now consists only of a church and a few houses and cottages. There are no ships in the river but many yachts, so many in fact that it is preferable if possible to avoid a visit in August week-ends and bank holidays.

The Approaches and Creeks

Newtown River lies on the Island shore, 3½ miles east of Yarmouth and seven cables ESE of Hamstead Ledge. The best time for a first visit is on a rising tide before the mud flats are covered and the trend of the channels can still be seen. At high water everything is covered and strangers often go aground despite the perches marking the mud.

Approaching from the west make Hamstead Ledge green conical buoy. Here the stream is very strong and the water rough if the wind is contrary to it. In good weather the buoy can be passed on the wrong side, leaving it a cable to port and crossing the ledges in over 3 fathoms. Then steer due east for ½ mile, when the small red spherical bar buoy will be close at hand.

From the eastward keep Yarmouth Pier well open of Hamstead Point to avoid Newtown Gravel Banks and leave the bar buoy to port. The entrance to the River and

4.1. Newtown entrance from seaward. The leading marks are indicated and therefore the bar buoy should be left well to port.

the leading marks will then be seen. The entrance lies between two shingle spits, at the east end of the shingle shore extending for ½ mile east of Hamstead Point, which is backed by a line of low trees for most of the distance. The leading marks consist of two beacon posts on the mud to the east of the entrance on the north side of Fishhouse Point. The outer one is painted with RW stripes and has a Y topmark and the inner bears a white disc within a black circle.

Bring these marks in line and stand in on their transit at approximately SE. The small spherical red bar buoy (but the bar is to the WSW of it) will be left nearly a cable to port.

4.2. The leading marks at low water. Fishhouse Point is on the extreme right.

4.3. The river entrance with Fishhouse Point on the left. The yacht aground in the centre indicates the shingle bank which dries out. It is marked by green perches, sometimes weathered, but, as can be seen, these should be given a wide berth. This picture, and those which follow, were taken at MLWS with an easterly wind and a low run of tide.

Continue on the transit leaving perches with red can topmarks to port and a small spherical green buoy to starboard, which marks the steep gravel bank on the west side. The outer leading beacon, which is near the edge of the channel, may be used as a port hand boom when bear to starboard to leave to port Fishhouse Point and two port hand perches close to it.

The bed of the channel is uneven, with only about 3 ft (0·9 m) on the bar, increasing to 5 ft (1·5 m) and then to 7 ft (2·1 m) and 11 ft (3·3 m) before falling to 4 ft (1·2 m) SW of Fishhouse Pt. It then deepens to 9 ft (2·7 m) before decreasing gradually to 3 ft (0·9 m) off the junction with Causeway Lake. It is marked by several perches on the mud on each side, those with red can topmarks to port and those to starboard painted green, though they sometimes become weathered so that the colours may not immediately be recognized. Occasionally they get knocked down or their position altered.

Just inside the entrance two drying shingle banks lie on the starboard side of the channel. Despite their being marked by two or three green perches, strangers often run aground here by steering direct towards yachts at anchor or on moorings and leaving the perches on the wrong side. As will be seen from the chart, after the entrance has been passed, there is a pronounced bend in the river. It runs SE towards a red port hand perch with a can top, on the north side of the entrance of Clamerkin Lake, before bending round to the SSW, in the reach where a number of yachts on moorings lie in the centre of the channel. Note that on the south side of the entrance to Clamerkin Lake there is a green perch, which is a starboard mark when entering this channel but must be left to port when continuing up Newtown River. The channel is then easier to follow close to the yachts at moorings as the deep water (varies between 6 ft and 4 ft (1·8 and 1·2 m)) is very narrow. Near the junction with Causeway Lake the depth falls to about 3 ft (0·9 m). Beyond this the water quickly shoals. At low tide there is little water in the upper tributaries, namely Western Haven and Shalfleet Lake: in fact, at low spring tides Shalfleet Lake dries out, although it is navigable at low water neap tides in a dinghy. The main arm of the harbour is only marked as far as the junction with Causeway Lake.

Clamerkin Lake is fairly deep, having over 4 ft (1·2 m) CD of water for a considerable distance. The channel is only marked by occasional perches but the line of yachts at anchor and moorings assists pilotage. There is danger from rifle practice at the top of the creek and in Spur Lake; red flags are flown during firing.

Lights: None in the river.

Moorings, Anchorage and Facilities

There is a good temporary anchorage during off-shore winds outside the river near the position marked 1·2 metres on the chart, or further outside, finding a suitable depth by taking soundings. This is now much used, especially at neaps when there is more water at low tide, if the river itself is crowded. The usual anchorage in the river is in about 9 ft to 6 ft (2·7 m to 1·8 m) in the first reach of the channel between the entrance and the permanent moorings belonging to local yachts—see over for possibility of hiring one. In strong northerly winds the entrance and anchorage can be rough near high water, especially on the first of the ebb at springs when the stream is strong. Better shelter is found farther up the river near the junction with Causeway Lake in about 3 ft (0·9 m) at CD plus $1\frac{1}{2}$ ft (0·5 m)

4.4. Looking up Newtown River. The yachts on moorings indicate the trend of the channel. The lower Hamstead landing is about two cables up on the starboard side.

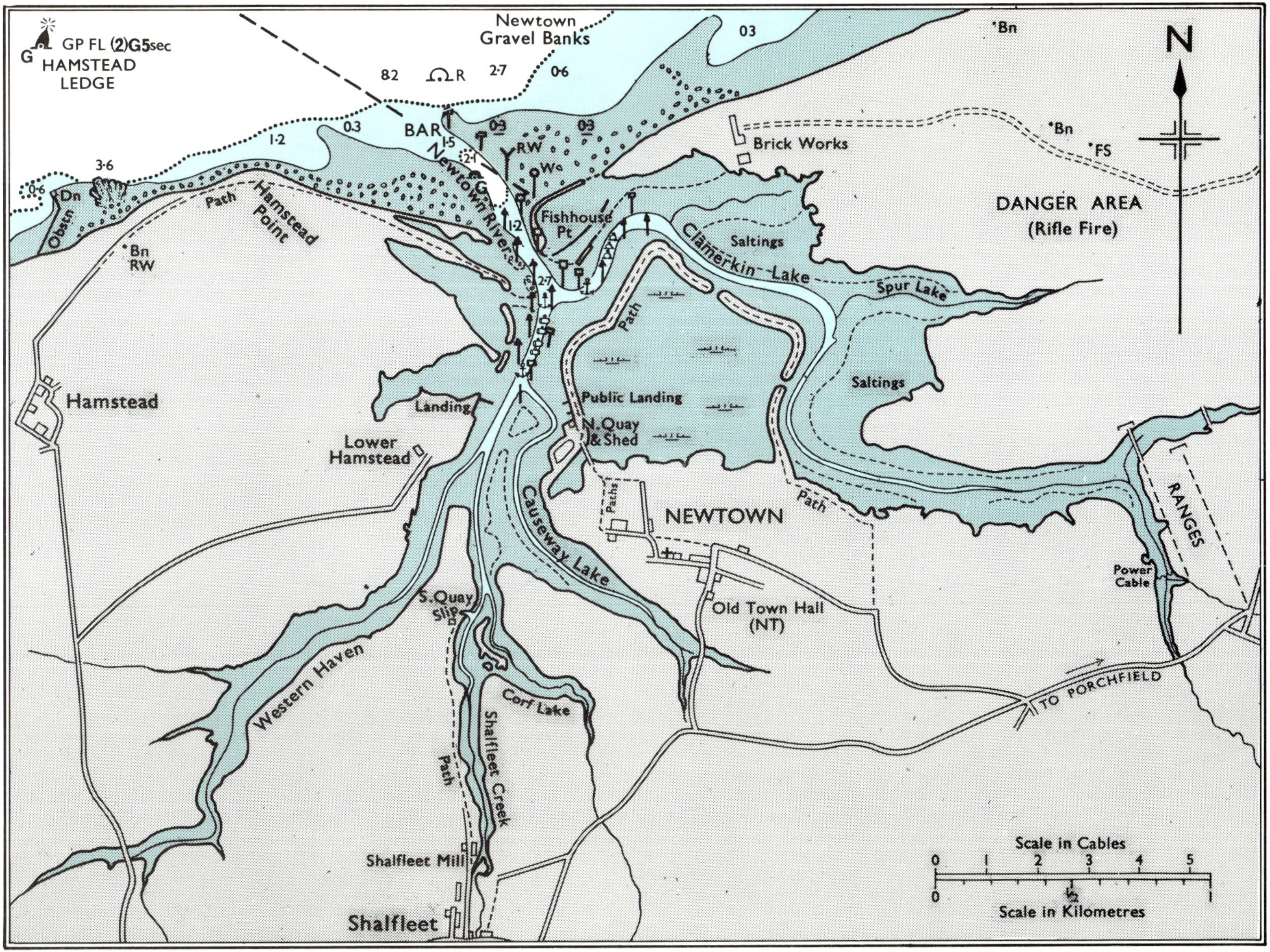
GP FL (2)G5sec
HAMSTEAD LEDGE
Newtown Gravel Banks
BAR
Newtown River
Fishhouse Pt
Brick Works
DANGER AREA
(Rifle Fire)
N
Saltings
Clamerkin Lake
Spur Lake
Saltings
Hamstead Point
Path
Hamstead
Landing
Lower Hamstead
Public Landing
N. Quay & Shed
Path
Paths
NEWTOWN
Path
RANGES
Power Cable
Causeway Lake
Old Town Hall (NT)
S. Quay Slip
Western Haven
Corf Lake
Shalfleet Creek
Path
TO PORCHFIELD
Shalfleet Mill
Shalfleet
Scale in Cables
Scale in Kilometres

4.5. The entrance to Causeway Lake, which is marked by perches, is about one cable to seaward of the Hamstead landing on the opposite side. In the background is the black shed and slip. The public landing place is about 100 yards to the left.

at MLWS or 4·8 ft (1·5 m) at MLWN, but the best positions are now occupied by permanent moorings. Centreboard or very light draft yachts, however, may be able to find snug anchorage beyond the permanent moorings and there is more water there at neap tides. There is also anchorage in 4 ft (1·2 m) CD (about 5½ or 6 ft at ordinary springs) in the first reach of Clamerkin Lake which in some respects is the best.

Yachts are requested not to anchor beyond the anchorage limits marked by notice boards, owing to the proximity of oyster beds in Clamerkin Lake and Newtown River. Anchors should be buoyed when anchoring near permanent moorings especially in the main arm.

There are three visitor's moorings (conspicuous white buoys) in Clamerking Lake and there are three more white buoys in the main arm leading to Shalfleet. Application should be made to the Berthing Master (Mr. B. Smith. Tel. Calbourne 424). He or his Deputy may be found at the black shed by the Quay. They visit yachts to collect harbour dues, which are payable for mooring or anchorage. They are well earned for without the River Committee there would, at times, be absolute chaos owing to too many yachts in too small an area. If they are not collected it is requested that any dues will be placed in the National Trust box behind the shed on the quay.

There is a public landing on the east side of the river north of the quay. Facilities for yachts are limited, which is perhaps a good thing as the charm of the creeks lies in the lack of development of the unspoilt countryside. Limited repairs can be undertaken by Mr. Richard Seabroke, who can be contacted at the Quay or at Marsh Farm (Calbourne 213)

Newtown River: Soundings in metre. Add 0·5 m (1·6 ft) at MLWS, 1·5 m (4·8 ft) at MLWN. Based on British Admiralty Chart No. 2040, with the permission HM Stationery Office and of the Hydrographer of the Navy.

4.6. The entrance of Clamerkin Lake. The perch on the drying bank is port hand (red with a can top) and should be given a wide berth. Behind it is another red port hand perch but looks green owing to weed.

which can be reached by footpath from the Quay. At Lower Hamstead on the west side of the river there is a private landing but yachtsmen are allowed to use it at their own risk. From the landing it is only 200 yards to the farm where water and groceries may be obtained as well as milk, butter and eggs. Alternatively, make a dinghy excursion to the quay by the old saltings in Shalfleet Lake; then follow the track along to the bank of the creek to Shalfleet on a main bus route, where there is the New Inn and a village shop which is nearly always open in summer. There is a small yacht yard (Mr. Woodford) and slip at Shalfleet Quay and near high water the creek is navigable by shoal draft yachts thus far. Apply at the yacht yard for a mooring of which there are a fair number in the reach off the quay for craft of shoal draft.

The creeks provide interesting sailing for dinghy excursions and there are many splendid walks, of which perhaps the best is to Upper Hamstead along the shore or the wooded bank where there is a profusion of primroses and violets in the spring, but adders have also been seen there. The whole estuary and much of the surrounding land is the property of the National Trust and it is requested that the Trust's bye-laws be observed. The land and marshes near the creeks provide nesting places for countless sea and water birds. During the nesting seasons April-June inclusive 'No Landing' notices are placed on Fishhouse Point and it is hoped that yachtsmen will co-operate in the preservation of the birds which add so much interest to the surroundings.

5 Beaulieu River

Double High Water at entrance: Springs −0 h 45 m Portsmouth and +1 h 20 m; Neaps mean +0 h 5 m.
Tidal Heights above datum at entrance approx: MHWS 12·2 ft (3·7 m) MLWS 1·9 ft (0·6 m) MHWN 10·2 ft (3·1 m) MLWN 5·2 ft (1·6 m).
Stream sets to the westward off East Lepe Buoy about −1 h 0 m Portsmouth, and to the eastward about +4 h 45 m Portsmouth.
Depths: Bar on leading line 2 ft (0·6 m) CD. The river bed is uneven with from a depth of 5 ft (1·5 m) up to 20 ft (6·0 m) as far as Buckler's Hard, except for a few shoaler patches referred to below.
Yacht Clubs: R Southampton YC, Beaulieu River SC.

Of all the Solent creeks and harbours Beaulieu River is undoubtedly the most beautiful. From the entrance its wide channel leads west between marshes, the sanctuary of sea birds, and then takes a turn to the northward bringing the yachtsman within the 'perambulations of the Forest'.

Buckler's Hard, situated on the west bank about half way up the river was established by John, Duke of Montagu, in the eighteenth century and became the scene of ship-building activities. In the wide street between the cottages and Buckler's Hard lay piled the Forest oak from which the wooden walls of Nelson's days were built. The house of Henry Adams, the famous shipbuilder, is still standing, and is now preserved as 'The Master Builder's House' hotel.

From Buckler's Hard the river pursues a wandering course through the Forest for two miles, drying out at low water in the last reach leading to Beaulieu. Here there is the historic abbey, believed to have been founded by King John and built by the Cistercian monks in the year 1204. The monks were given a charter with the maximum possible privileges, which tradition attributes to the consequence of the King's bad dream after he had ordered his servants to trample certain monks under the feet of their horses. In more recent times the ancient rights of the monks, confirmed by various sovereigns to the successive owners of Beaulieu, were inherited by Lord Montagu and the Trustees of the Beaulieu Estate. These rights, almost without parallel in the British Isles, include ownership of the bed of the river and foreshore, flotsam, jetsam, lagan and wreck. From the yachtsmen's point of view the landowner's rights have been an advantage. They have prevented unsightly development and, besides keeping the river unspoilt, have led to the entrance and channel being properly boomed and the appointment of a Harbour Master who is most helpful to visiting yachtsmen, besides collecting the dues.

The Approach, Entrance and Channel

Approaching the entrance from the westward keep well off shore to avoid the shallow water off the Warren Flat and Beaulieu Spit until the conspicuous coastguard cottages, a white boathouse and the conspicuous tripod dolphin (which bears a light

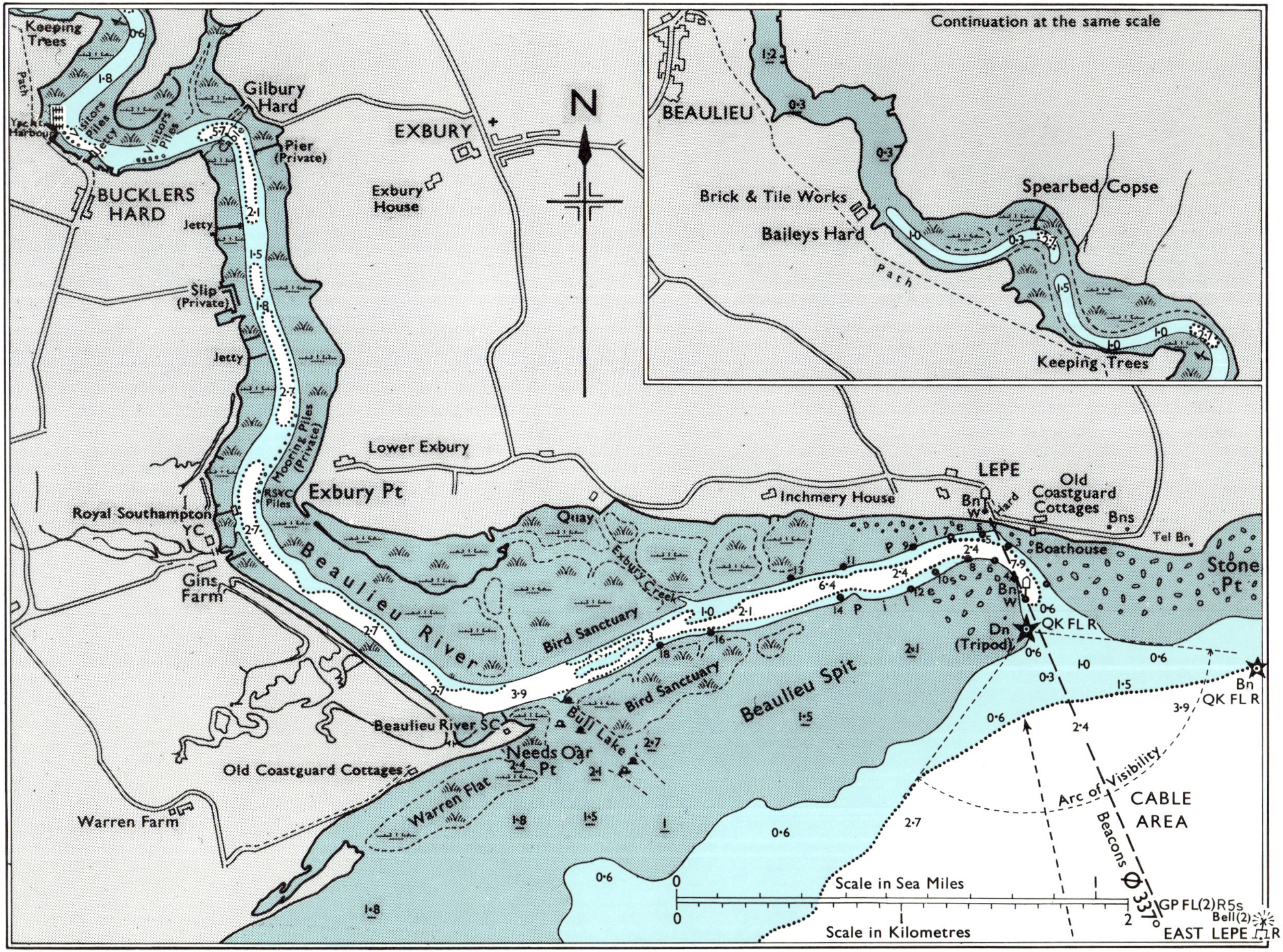
Continuation at the same scale
BEAULIEU
Brick & Tile Works
Baileys Hard
Spearbed Copse
Keeping Trees
Path
N
Keeping Trees
Path
Yacht Harbour
Visitors Piles
Jetty
Gilbury Hard
Pier (Private)
EXBURY
Exbury House
BUCKLERS HARD
Jetty
Slip (Private)
Jetty
Mooring Piles (Private)
RSYC Piles
Lower Exbury
Exbury Pt
Royal Southampton YC
Gins Farm
Beaulieu River
Quay
Exbury Creek
Bird Sanctuary
Bird Sanctuary
Inchmery House
LEPE
Old Coastguard Cottages
Bns
Tel Bn
Boathouse
Stone Pt
Hard
Bn W
Dn (Tripod)
QK FL R
Bn QK FL R
Beaulieu Spit
Beaulieu River SC
Bull Lake
Needs Oar Pt
Old Coastguard Cottages
Warren Flat
Warren Farm
Arc of Visibility
CABLE AREA
Beacons Φ 337°
Scale in Sea Miles
Scale in Kilometres
GP FL(2)R5s
Bell(2)
EAST LEPE R

Qk Fl R and a notice limiting speed to 5 knots) are identified and the entrance is opened up. The dolphin marks the west side of the entrance and stands in shallow water at the eastern end of Beaulieu Spit, which covers on the last quarter of the flood. The front leading mark has a white board with an angular top on the first port hand pile and the rear is a similar white mark on a pole. The latter is not so clear as it is among trees situated about 1½ cables west of the conspicuous ex-coastguard cottages and white boathouse on the shore. Bring the leading marks into line at 337° and stand in on their transit, which leaves the dolphin about ½ cable to port.

When approaching Beaulieu River from the eastward keep well clear of the shoals between Stansore Pt and Stone Pt, marked by three beacons (*Qk Fl R*) situated near the fathom (1·8 m) line. See page 59 for information on cable area. Shoal water continues to extend about 3 cables from the shore west of the beacons, and it is simplest after passing the most westerly beacon to bring it into line with the middle beacon and sail on this stern transit until the leading marks for the river are brought into line, when proceed as before.

The transit of the leading marks at 337° leads on the extreme west side of the entrance channel so it is best to open the shore beacon slightly to the east. There is only about 2 ft (0·6 m) at CD (4 ft MLWS) on the bar east of the tripod beacon, but the depth increases to 7 ft (2·1 m) and soon to over 20 ft (6·0 m) after the first leading mark is passed. The channel is clearly marked by piles with reflectors. On the port hand these are red piles (even numbers) with can tops and red reflectors and on the starboard hand green piles (odd numbers) with green conical tops and green reflectors. Booms and perches are placed on the edge of the mud and should not be approached closely.

As the shore is approached the entrance channel bends round to the west behind Beaulieu Spit into a long straight reach between mud banks on either side. The accompanying chart shows some of the depths in this first reach which carries a least depth of 7 ft (2·1 m) except for a 3 ft (1·0 m) shoal on the north side of the channel at the entrance of the Exbury Creek and a middle ground 2 cables beyond it. The latter is shown on official charts as drying out at CD but locally it is said that there is rarely less than 4 ft (1·2 m) water over it.

The river begins to bend again off the jetty of the Beaulieu River SC at Need's Oar Point, turning to the NW and leading past Gin's Farm and the R Southampton YC. This reach is deep except in vicinity of a shoal on the east side shown on the chart and a shoal on the west side off Gin's Farm, where there is a hard and a private pier. A cable beyond this is the jetty and pontoon of the R Southampton YC, and the pile moorings reserved for the club. Here the river bends to NNE and then to N for the mile reach up to Gilbury Hard. The channel is wide and clear with a least depth of 5 ft (1·5 m) at CD but is 7 ft (2·1 m) and over for the most part. Off Gilbury Hard it turns sharply to the westward up to Buckler's Hard east of which there is a shoal stated to be rarely less than 4 ft. Above Buckler's Hard the depths vary considerably from 3 ft (0·9 m) to 9 ft (2·7 m)

Beaulieu River: Soundings in metres. Add 0·5 m (1·6 ft) at MLWS, 1·5 m (4·8 ft) at MLWN. Based on British Admiralty Chart No. 2040, with the permission of HM Stationery Office and of the Hydrographer of the Navy.

as far as the pier at Spearbed Copse, and the channel is navigable with sufficient rise of tide as far as the brickworks at Bailey's Hard where there is a landing. Beyond this the river dries out at CD, though it can be used by light draft craft near high water up to Timbrell's Quay at Beaulieu. All the jetties on the river are private, but in addition to the hards mentioned there are landings at Gilbury Hard, a cable beyond the jetty, (Gilbury village and stores $\frac{3}{4}$ mile walk) and at Keeping Trees, $\frac{1}{2}$ mile above Buckler's Hard.

Light: A light, *Qk Fl R* which must not be confused with the *Qk Fl R* lights on the three beacons off Stone Pt, is established on the outer tripod dolphin. This enables the river to be used at night with local knowledge, and given clear moonlight possibly also by strangers.

Bull Lake (or Bull Run): This swatchway just east of Need's Oar Point from the Solent into Beaulieu River has always been used by yachtsmen with local knowledge and with sufficient rise of tide. It is now well marked by buoys from 1st April to 1st November and provides a useful short cut when coming from the west.

The approach lies from approximately $\frac{1}{2}$ mile SE of the extremity of Need's Oar Point when the buoys will be seen. These are small round ones, 2 red to port and 3 over-painted black to starboard. The swatch dries out completely at low water springs on a bottom of gravel, small stones or mud. It can only be approached with sufficient rise of tide as shoal water extends a long way seawards of the buoys. The approach may best be made with Need's Oar Pt bearing about NW with the swatch open between the buoys. Short cuts from east or west direct to the outer buoys should not be made except by shoal draft craft. Allowance should be made for the cross stream in the offing. There is about 8 ft (2·4 m) at HW springs. At the inner end of the channel, on the east side where it joins the river, there is a tide gauge showing the depth of water in the swatch. For this

5.1. Beaulieu River entrance looking north showing from the left the dolphin at the entrance with the red Qk Fl light, the two leading marks, the back one partly hidden in the trees and the coastguard cottages on the right. The dolphin is left about ½ cable to port.

5.2. A nearer view of the leading marks.

reason it is much easier to use this short cut for the first time when *leaving* rather than entering the river. At HW the ebb stream in the swatch is strong as, when the stream turns west in the Solent, it runs at first into the entrance of Beaulieu River and out again through Bull Lake to rejoin the main Solent ebb.

Moorings, Anchorage and Facilities

Beaulieu River is one of the few remaining places in the Solent where it is still possible for yachts to anchor. This is permitted in the first long reach between Lepe House and Need's Oar Pt, which provides over a mile of water sheltered by land on the north side and on the south by Beaulieu Spit, except for a swell at the eastern end at HW

5.3. Looking out through the Bull Run from the river near the Beaulieu River Sailing Club.

in strong southerly winds. Nearest landings are on the beach at the entrance, at the quay up Exbury creek, which dries at half tide, and at Need's Oar, where the club house of the Beaulieu River SC is nearby. The anchorage is far from facilities but the 2 miles up the river to Buckler's Hard do not take long with the aid of an outboard engine. A riding light is advisable as the channel is used at night. Anchorage outside is prohibited in the cable area as indicated on the chart.

The moorings in the river are all privately rented, but there are pile moorings to accommodate about 100 visiting yachts. Application for a berth, or for the use of a mooring if temporarily available should be made to the Harbour Master at Buckler's Hard (Mr W. Grindley, Tel: Bucklers Hard 200). His office is at the Yacht Harbour. The Yacht Harbour marina is only a cable above the Buckler's Hard jetty. Here there are berths for 76 yachts. Fuel of all kinds and water can be had at the marina fuelling jetty. All facilities are provided including a yacht yard, chandlery shop and large car park.

In the small village, which consists of two widely spaced rows of cottages running down to the river, there is the Master Builder's House Hotel with restaurant and snack bar. The Maritime Museum (which is well worth seeing) is at the far end on the left, where there is the car park and Mulberry Tea Garden for light lunches and snacks. There is a good village stores, open every day in summer, and a garage with taxi service (Mr W. H. Martin, Tel: Buckler's Hard 249). Buses to Beaulieu and Southampton, Tuesday and Saturday, but the nearest station is Beaulieu Road 6 miles. A footpath provides a pleasant walk along the river and through the woods to Beaulieu.

At Beaulieu landing can be made at high water where there is 5 ft (1·5 m) at Timbrell's Quay, where there is the Palace Quay boatyard, and light boats can be launched. The Abbey and Palace House and gardens and Motor Museum are open to visitors and there are a few shops, PO and an hotel.

5.5. Buckler's Hard. The Yacht Harbour is about a cable beyond the jetty.

5.4. Gin's Farm and private landing.
To the right is the Royal Southampton Yacht Club
but the club's landing is just out
of the picture.

6 Cowes and Medina River

High Water (Long): Springs mean −0 h 15 m Portsmouth; Neaps mean +0 h 15 m.
Tidal Heights: MHWS 13·9 ft (4·2 m), MLWS 1·9 ft (0·6 m), MHWN 11·4 ft (3·3 m), MLWN 5·6 ft (1·7 m).
Stream sets to the westward in Cowes Roads 1 h 30 m before local HW and to the eastward just before LW.
Depths: Except for a 5 ft (1·5 m) patch opposite East Cowes SC, there is a minimum of 8 ft (2·4 m) in the channel to within ½ mile of the Folly Inn, when depths fall to 3 ft (0·9 m) and then to 1 ft (0·3 m) off the light beacon, beyond which the channel soon dries out.
Yacht Clubs: Royal Yacht Squadron, Royal London Yacht Club, Royal Corinthian Yacht Club, Island Sailing Club, East Cowes Sailing Club, Cowes Corinthian Yacht Club, Gurnard Sailing Club.

The days of the great schooners and cutters, with their famous owners and big professional crews, are long past and with them something of the splendour of Cowes has gone. Today the scene is basically amateur but infinitely broader and more active with the vast fleets of smaller yachts. Cowes Week, when coupled with the start of the Fastnet Race, provides the highlight which attracts yachtsmen the world over and creates what is probably the greatest and most vivid spectacle in International yacht racing.

Cowes is conveniently centred near the middle of the Island shore and at no time in its history has the town been more dedicated to yachting and providing amenities for visiting yachtsmen.

Approach and Entrance

Approach from the west is easy by following the line of the coast from Egypt Point about a cable offshore or less according to the state of the tide and draft of the yacht. As racing men know, sometimes to their cost, there are rocky ledges extending in places almost ½ cable seawards. The streams are strong. When approaching from the west, or leaving the harbour bound west, an early eddy running contrary to the main flood stream will be found inshore between the Squadron and Egypt Point.

From the eastward keep well to seaward to avoid the Shrape Mud and shallow water north and NW of it. At night a look out should be kept for unlit buoys.

The fairway lies on the west side of the harbour and is marked by buoys. On the east side there is a long breakwater which serves to scour the tide and to provide protection from winds from this quarter. On this side the water is shallow but at ordinary springs there is 2 ft (0·6 m) and at neaps 5½ ft (1·7 m) more than is shown on the chart. The area is occupied by large numbers of private moorings and if sailing among them care should be taken to avoid being set by the stream on to moored yachts. Caution must also be exercised if crossing the Hovercraft channel, which rounds the end of the breakwater as shown on the accompanying chart and is marked by unlit orange fluorescent buoys on the starboard side when approaching from the seaward end.

Parts of the fairway may be busy with racing craft on big regatta days which, by

6.1. The Royal Yacht Squadron Castle and Cowes foreshore towards Egypt Point.

courtesy, should be given right-of-way, especially as seconds count when they are working into position for the start of a race or approaching the finishing line. Red Funnel ferries and ships add to the congestion despite the care and consideration with which they are handled, but the channel is easy to follow past the Island Sailing Club, the Red Funnel pontoon, the marina and visitors' moorings. The channel narrows where the floating bridge chain ferry crosses it—and note that the chains lie at least 2 ft (0·6 m) above the bottom in mid-channel. Near the floating bridge and for a good $\frac{1}{4}$ mile beyond it the wind is often flukey owing to high ground and proximity of buildings. Beyond the chain ferry there are no navigation buoys but the deep water lies in the area between the pile mooring trots and heavy moorings. Except for the patch shown on the chart opposite the East Cowes SC, the minimum depth is 8 ft (2·4 m) to within $\frac{1}{2}$ mile (1 km) of the Folly Inn. *See River Medina.*

The maximum speed permitted for all vessels within Cowes Harbour is 6 knots over the ground, but speed should be reduced in the vicinity of yachts on moorings or as seamanship requires. Water ski-ing or planing is prohibited.

Lights: The Prince Consort buoy, situated about $\frac{1}{2}$ mile NE of the entrance exhibits a *V Qk Fl* light and port hand No 4 buoy is *Fl R ev 5 sec*. The light on the end of the breakwater is *Qk Fl R*. The leading lights in transit at 164° consist of a white light (*Iso 2 sec 6 miles*) on the post at the seaward end of Watch House landing and a rear light (*Iso Red*

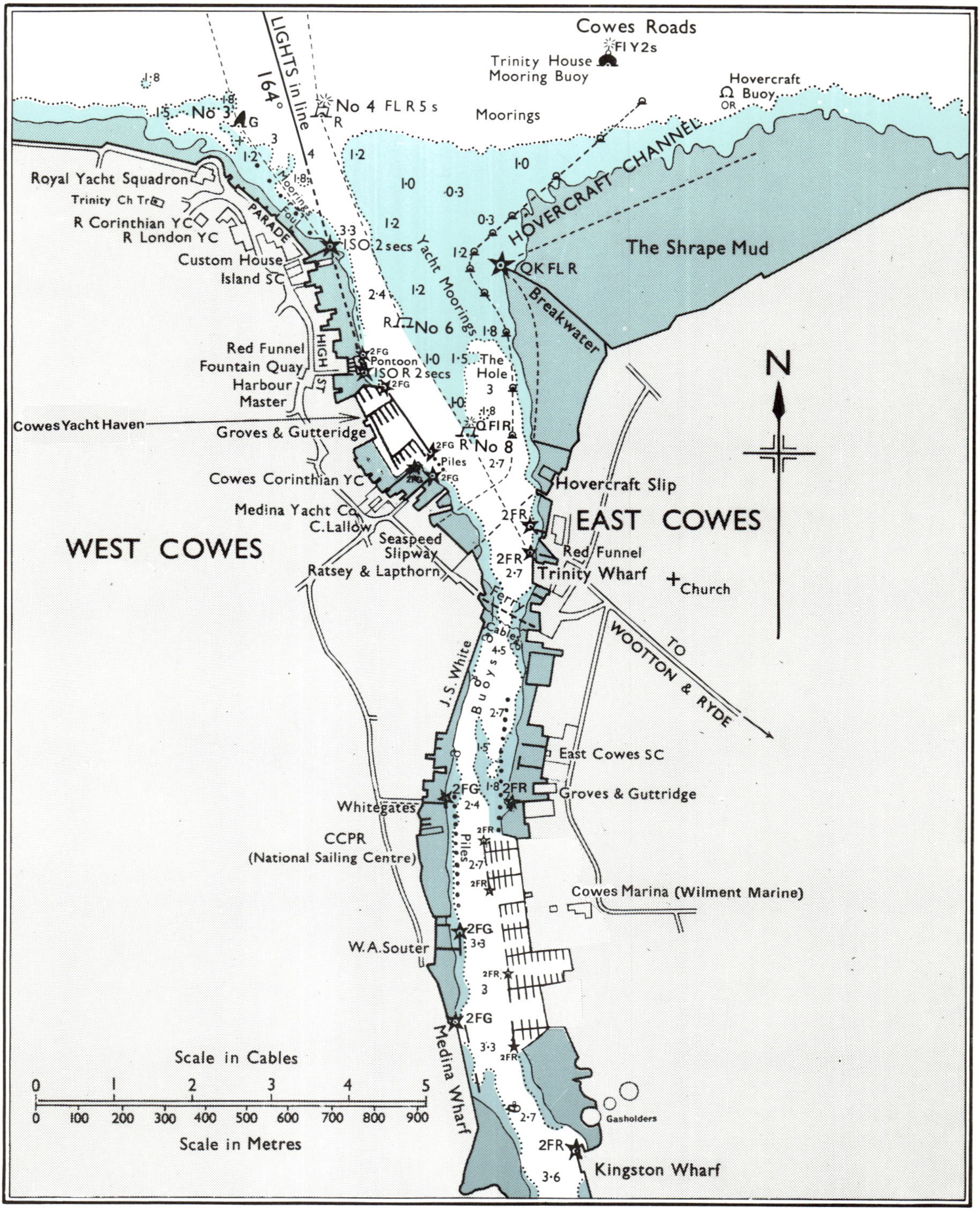

Cowes: Soundings in metres. Add 0·6 m (1·9 ft) at MLWS, 1·7 m (5·6 ft) at MLWN. Based on British Admiralty Chart No. 2793, with the permission of HM Stationery Office and of the Hydrographer of the Navy.

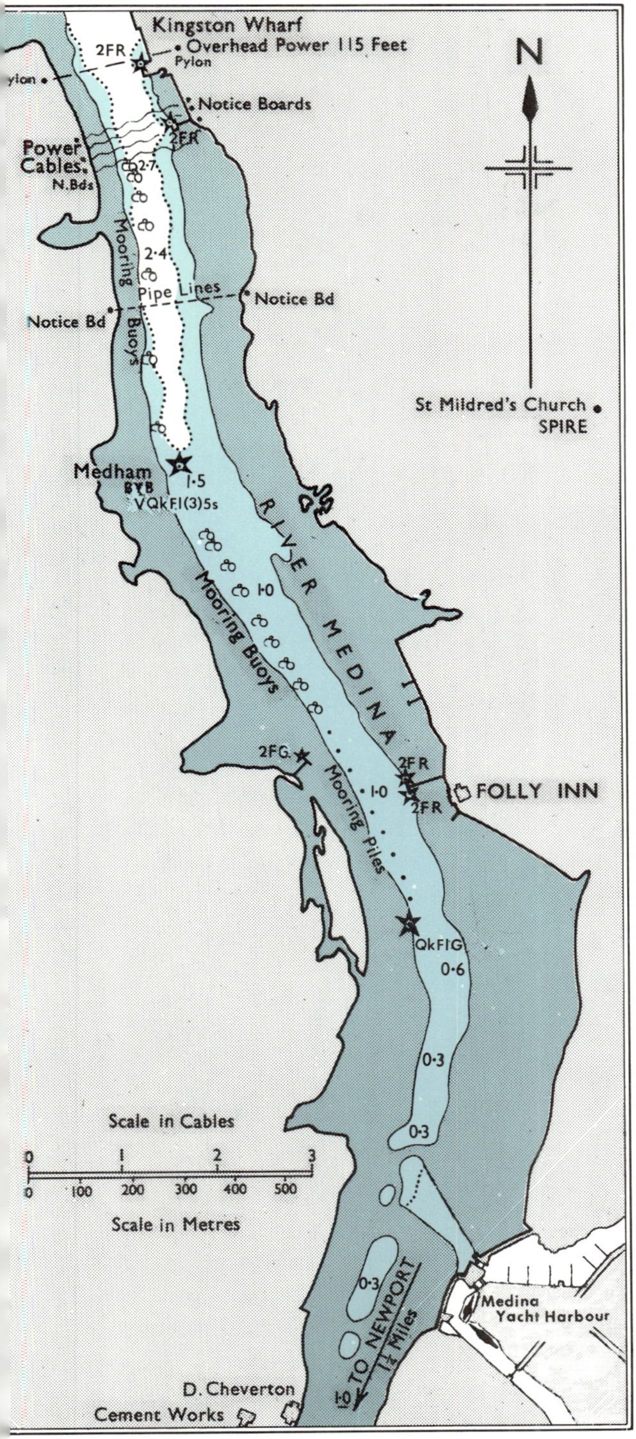

2 sec 3 miles) on the Dolphin on the south side of Fountain Pier. There are fixed red (to port) and green (to starboard) lights on the various wharfs and pontoons and up the river there is a *V Qk Fl (3) 5s* light on Medham beacon and a *Qk Fl G* light on the beacon south of the Folly Inn.

Moorings and Anchorages

There are four large temporary visitors' moorings situated off the Parade, on the starboard hand just past the Royal Yacht Squadron, convenient for Customs clearance. The Cowes Yacht Haven lies on the starboard hand just beyond the Fountain Pier and the Red Funnel Pontoon in the area previously occupied by mooring piles. This marina welcomes and provides for visiting yachtsmen, even those staying only overnight. Yachts berth alongside floating pontoons close to the centre of the town and facilities, but two pile berths where yachts moor abreast of each other remain available just south of the marina.

The swinging moorings on the east side of the harbour are private, or specially laid for racing classes during regattas, and must not be picked up by visitors, though it is sometimes possible to obtain the temporary use of one on application to the Harbour Master, Capt H. N. J. Wrigley, Tel: Cowes 3952.

Medina River: Soundings in metres. Add 0·7 m (2·5 ft) at MLWS, 1·7 m (5·7 ft) at MLWN. Based on British Admiralty Chart No. 2793, with the permission of HM Stationery Office and of the Hydrographer of the Navy.

6.2. Cowes front looking seaward. The Island Sailing Club and pontoon is in the foreground with the customs office just beyond it. The prominent white building is Osborne Court flats and the Royal Yacht Squadron is on the extreme right.

As the harbour is exposed to all northerly winds it can be very uncomfortable in strong winds and gales from this quarter, when it may be better to move up the river. Visitors moorings (clearly marked by notice boards) will be found there on both sides of the river on piles in the reach to the south of the floating bridge to suit any size of yacht. The Cowes Marina, built by Wilment Marine, has visitors' berths at East Cowes some three cables above the chain ferry ('floating bridge') on the east bank of the river. There are also pile moorings for small visiting yachts in the Folly reach, opposite the Folly Inn. Beyond them is the Medina Yacht Harbour—see River Medina.

Anchorage is to seaward of existing mooring buoys which lie between No 4 R buoy and the Hovercraft buoys. Cowes Roads are exposed and the streams through them are strong so the anchorage is used mostly by larger yachts. Smaller craft usually anchor in shallower water, with the help of soundings, closer in to the north and NW of the end of the breakwater where there is plenty of water at neaps clear of the Hovercraft channel. In settled weather and offshore winds, anchorage is possible, but not recommended, off the Parade to the west of the Squadron, a position which is not far from the town though subject to the swell from passing ships.

Anchors should be buoyed anywhere in the vicinity of Cowes in case of fouling mooring chains, particularly those of big commercial buoys which often stretch a long distance. In fact, the chains of the Trinity House mooring buoy, for example, extend 500 ft east and west, though in the harbour the scope is much shorter. Anchorage is prohibited (1) in the fairway (2) in the Hovercraft channel and the mooring area on the east side of the harbour (3) where there are cables or obstructions indicated by notice boards such as just beyond the floating bridge or off Kingston Power station (4) in the Folly Reach.

Facilities

There are many public landings among which the following may be mentioned in order of approach: several on the Parade, Watch House Slip (nearest to Customs) two farther south leading to High Street, south side Fountain pontoon and other landings south of it. Whitegates pontoon is the most convenient beyond the Floating bridge and just beyond it is the National Sailing Centre pontoon. Landing is also possible by permission at various yacht yards. At East Cowes there are three slipways but at present no convenient hards or pontoons.

As stated before, Cowes is dedicated to yachting and provides exceptionally good facilities of all kinds within easy distance of the harbour. There are no less than seven yacht clubs, including the Royal Yacht Squadron which remains the premier yacht club and the Island Sailing Club, which is very go-ahead and has excellent facilities with a pontoon in the season for members and visiting yachtsmen introduced by members. It is hospitable towards foreign yachtsmen, especially to visitors in Cowes Week.

6.3. The Cowes Yacht Haven.

Cowes and Medina River

Yacht building and repairs are undertaken at Lallow's, Souter's, Groves & Guttridge and several other yards. Fuel and water available at Lallow's and Souter's jetties and other yacht yards. There are also fresh water points at Watch House slipway, Whitegates pontoon and Old Town Quay. Among the well known names in the yachting industry are Ratsey & Lapthorn (sails), Beken's (photographs), Pascall Atkeys and the Foredeck (chandlers), Bannister (ropes), Henderson (pumps), Benzie (yachting jewellery) and Morgans (outfitters). In addition there are engineers and riggers and pretty well any yachting requirement is available. EC Wednesday. Customs at Watch House slip and bonded stores from Shergold's. The best known hotels with restaurants are the Gloster and the Fountain, but there are several others and numerous pubs and boarding houses. Cowes is a convenient harbour in which to leave a yacht under surveillance during an owner's absence by arrangement with the Harbour Master.

There is a good bus service connecting with all parts of the Island. Red Funnel steamers to Southampton regularly. British Rail Seaspeed hovercraft and Red Funnel Seaflight hydrofoil services to Southampton.

RIVER MEDINA

The river cuts a long groove through to the centre of the Island from Cowes to Newport, the capital. It is in part commercial, but the land in the background on either side is high and to the east it is well wooded so the scene is by no means unattractive. The channel is not buoyed but it lies between mooring piles or mooring buoys and it is not difficult to follow with depths of 8 ft (2·4 m) to Kingston Power Station and ¼ mile beyond, when it becomes shallower and soon falls to 3 ft (0·9 m) as the Folly reach is entered. The river is spanned by an overhead power cable (height 115 ft—35 m) at

6.4. The Folly Inn and public landing with dinghy pontoons on the east bank of the Medina River.

6.5. The entrance to the Medina Yacht Harbour on the east bank above the Folly Inn.

Kingston and by submarine power cables and a pipe line, the positions being marked by notice boards to indicate prohibited anchorage.

From Kingston to the Folly Inn the channel is best followed by leaving the line of moorings and Medham Beacon close to starboard. On an ordinary spring tide yachts of 5 ft (1·5 m) draft can sail up to the Folly Point and there is plenty of water at neaps, though larger yachts should bring up to the piles in 6 ft (1·8 m) to 8 ft (2·4 m) about ½ mile to the northward.

Off the Folly Inn there are pile moorings suitable at ordinary springs for yachts drawing 4½ ft (1·4 m) or, say, 7 ft to 8 ft (1·8 m to 2·4 m) at neaps, but anchorage is not permitted. There is a landing pontoon at the jetty and a scrubbing hard which can be used by arrangement at the inn, where there is a buffet bar and meals can be had to order. Fresh water is laid to the pontoon and there is a small shop. Calor gas is available. In all, it is a quiet and pleasant place to bring up, and there is a path along the river bank the whole way to Newport.

The Medina Yacht Harbour (ex Medway Queen Marina) lies about 4 cables South of the Folly Inn with berths for 240 yachts in the locked basin. The approach channel marked by port hand piles and starboard buoys is dredged to 3 ft (0·9 m) MLWS. The depth in the basin is maintained at about 8 ft (2·4 m). The lock is operated on request 3 hours either side of high water when 8 ft (2·4 m) of water will be found. It is not normally lit but can be flood-lit if a yacht is expected at night. Manager: Paul Merritt. Tel: Newport 526733.

Above the Folly the depths soon begin to decrease but the river is navigable with sufficient rise of tide by ships to Newport docks. The upper reaches provide interesting sailing, with dinghy landing at Newport (EC Thursday) on the port side above the old railway bridge.

7 Southampton Water

Double High Water: Springs −0 h 30 m and +1 h 30 m Portsmouth; Neaps mean +0 h 15 m. At Springs after about 3 hours flood there is a stand for 1½ hours, followed by a 3½ hours rise. The ebb runs strongly for 3½ hours attaining maximum rate 2 hours after second HW.
Tidal Heights: Southampton, above datum. MHWS 15 ft (4·6 m) MLWS 1·5 ft (0·5 m) MHWN 11·3 ft (3·9 m) MLWN 5·8 ft (1·9 m).
Depths: Ample at any state of the tide.
Yacht Clubs: R Southampton YC, Southampton SC, Ashlett SC, Eling SC, Hythe SC, Marchwood YC, Netley Cliff SC, Weston SC.

With its deep and easy approach and double high water Southampton has been a natural port and centre of shipbuilding from time immemorial. Inevitably too, it has been an objective of raids from the sea by Danes and the French. Nevertheless, it was the Norman Conquest which brought greatly increased trade to Southampton. The Bargate was built and the prosperous part of the town lay between this and the present Royal Pier, where some of it is still to be seen. The Middle Ages brought increased prosperity especially in the wool and wine trades. It was not until the middle of the eighteenth century that the port began its modern development and from then onwards grew rapidly in stature.

In particular, the name of Southampton has been linked with those of the great transatlantic liners. It was the home port of many famous ships, among which were the ill-fated *Titanic*, the *Mauretania* and *Lusitania* and the Queens, *Mary*, *Elizabeth* and *Elizabeth II*, besides their competitors among the great ships of the world seeking the honour of the Blue Riband. Passenger liners feature less in the news today, but Southampton remains a port for many of the leading passenger lines. The importance of the port has greatly increased in recent years by the expansion of the huge oil refinery at Fawley, the petroleum terminal on the opposite side of Southampton Water and by the regular car ferries to France and Spain and the development of container traffic.

Southampton Water provides a considerable length for day cruising with the added interest of its shipping. The port itself and the city are the administrative centre of the whole area, with the offices of the British Transport Docks Board, Customs, Lloyds Surveyors and the Ministry of Transport for the registration of yachts as well as of ships. The town offers every kind of yachting facility.

The Approach and Channel

Southampton Water and its approaches are wide and deep, and very well marked, so that the only point in navigation lies in keeping clear of the shipping in the fairways. The Southampton Dock Board southern boundary line runs from Stansore Point to Hill Head and there is a port bye-law which reads: 'Sailing vessels must not make use of the

7.1. Calshot Spit Light Vessel taken from the south-east.

deep water channel in such a way as to cause obstruction to the large steam vessels using the Port.' Another bye-law prohibits anchorage in the fairway and includes the Test and Itchen. The bye-laws should be strictly observed, as apart from the law, it is only common sense to keep out of the way of vessels, particularly tankers, which are very difficult to manoeuvre in the narrow water available for their deep draft, and which are virtually impossible to stop quickly.

So far as yacht racing is concerned the problem has to some extent been relieved by the laying of special buoys, which provide turning-marks clear of the deep channels. These are the Bald Head, Chilling, Clipper, East and West Knoll, Spanker and other buoys, which are laid in the summer months only and are shown on the accompanying chart. The problem should be a lesser one when cruising, as there is plenty of room in the approaches to Southampton to navigate either outside the deep fairways or on the edge of them without obstructing the big ships, crossing the fairways only when the channel is clear. What is important is to anticipate the movements of the big ships. Leaving Southampton Water and rounding usually close east of Calshot Light Vessel, they proceed down the Western Approach Channel. Thence they continue either in deep water west to

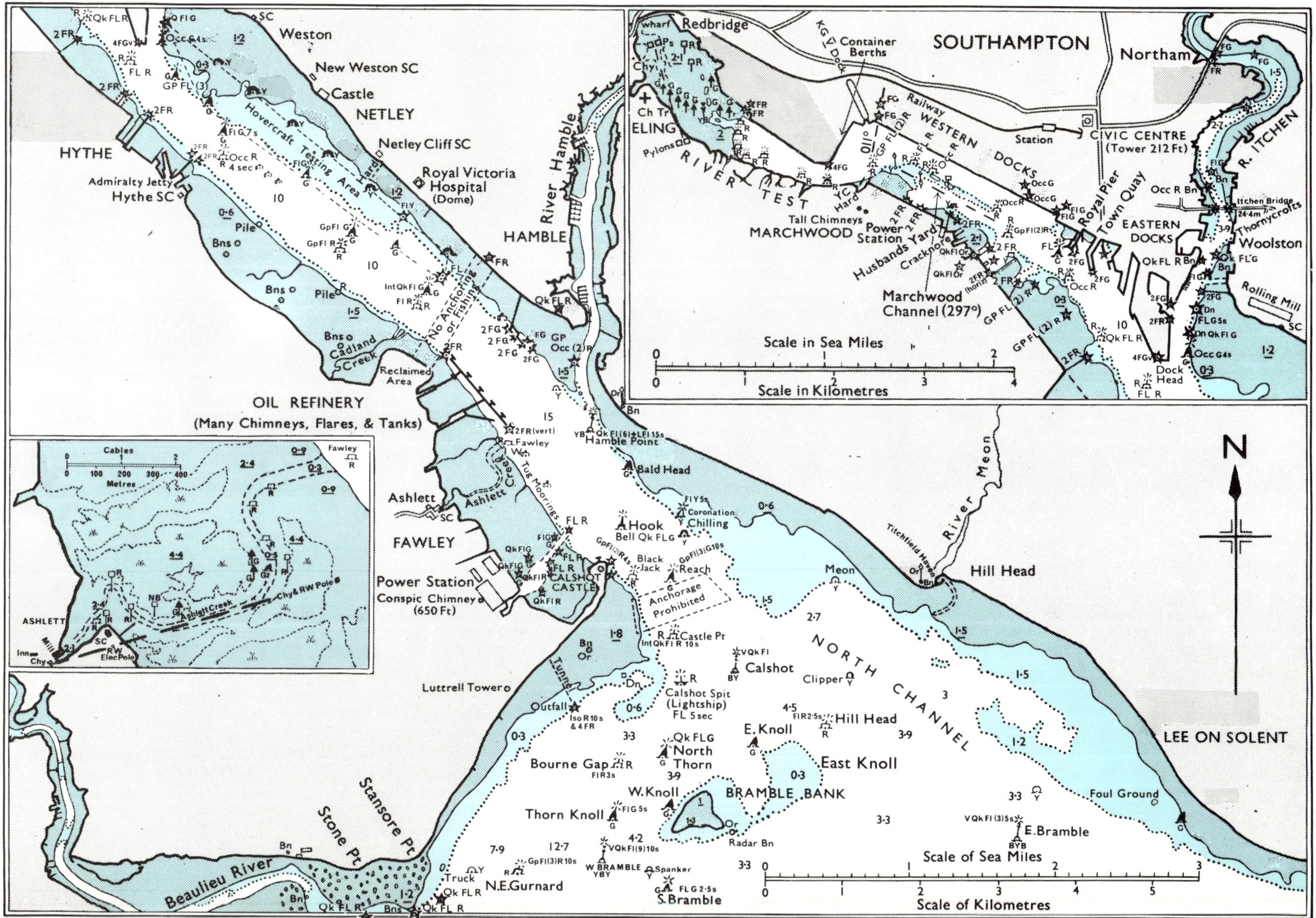

SOUTHAMPTON
Redbridge
Container Berths
K G V Dock
Northam
CIVIC CENTRE (Tower 212 Ft)
Station
Railway
WESTERN DOCKS
R. ITCHEN
Itchen Bridge
Thornycrofts
Woolston
Rolling Mill
EASTERN DOCKS
Royal Pier
Town Quay
Dock Head
ELING
Pylons
RIVER TEST
Tall Chimneys
MARCHWOOD
Power Station
Husbands Yard
Cracknore
Marchwood Channel (297°)
Scale in Sea Miles
Scale in Kilometres
HYTHE
Admiralty Jetty
Hythe SC
Weston
New Weston SC
Castle
NETLEY
Netley Cliff SC
Royal Victoria Hospital (Dome)
Hovercraft Testing Area
HAMBLE
River Hamble
No Anchoring or Fishing
Cadland Creek
Reclaimed Area
OIL REFINERY
(Many Chimneys, Flares, & Tanks)
Hamble Point
Bald Head
Fawley
Tug Moorings
Ashlett Creek
Ashlett
FAWLEY
Power Station
Conspic Chimney (650 Ft)
Hook
Coronation
Chilling
Black Jack
Reach
Anchorage Prohibited
CALSHOT CASTLE
Castle Pt
Calshot
Calshot Spit (Lightship) FL 5sec
Luttrell Tower
Tunnel
Outfall
Bourne Gap
North Thorn
E. Knoll
W. Knoll
Thorn Knoll
BRAMBLE BANK
East Knoll
Hill Head
Clipper
Meon
NORTH CHANNEL
Titchfield Haven
River Meon
Hill Head
LEE ON SOLENT
Foul Ground
E.Bramble
Radar Bn
W BRAMBLE
Spanker
S.Bramble
N.E.Gurnard
Truck
Stansore Pt
Stone Pt
Beaulieu River
Scale of Sea Miles
Scale of Kilometres
N
Cables
Metres
ASHLETT
Ashlett Creek
Chy & RW Pole
Elec Pole
Mill
Inn

the Needles (Signal W over Answering pennant) or they round the West Bramble bell buoy, turning to pass between the South Bramble and Prince Consort Buoy and east to Spithead. (Signal E over Answering pennant). Smaller ships may proceed east via the North Channel. When a ship is not under command or unable to avoid an approaching vessel 'she shall sound one long blast followed by two short blasts so that the approaching vessel can take action to avoid collision'.

Approaching from the west a good offing should be given to the shoals off Stone and Stansore Points, leaving to port three beacons, *Qk Fl R*, situated near the 1 fathom (1·8 m) line. Do not steer direct from the westerly beacon to the next at LW as the shoal bulges about 50 yards seaward between them. Power cables (from 33,000 to 132,000 volts), telephone cables and gas pipes cross the Solent from shore to shore in this prohibited anchorage, which extends approximately from Lepe to Gurnard Head on the west side and between Stansore Point and Egypt Point on the east. Damage can be caused even by a small yacht attempting to winch up an anchor fouled on a cable or by impact or grounding on a cable in shallow water such as lies northward of the three beacons. The owner of a yacht causing damage to a cable may render himself liable for loss and repair costs running into a very large sum.

The Western Approach for big ships lies between the flats off the Hampshire coast and the Bramble Bank. On the NW side it is marked by NE Gurnard buoy (*Gp Fl (3) R 10s*) and Bourne Gap buoy (*Fl R 3s*) and Calshot Spit light-vessel (*Fl 5s Horn (2)*) There is plenty of water for most yachts west of the buoys as shown on the chart, but Calshot Spit dries out in a SE direction for ½ mile from the beach and most Solent yachts leave the light-vessel about a cable and Castle Point buoy (*Int Qk Fl R 10s*) ½ cable to starboard, which gives 5 ft at MLWS. Greater liberties can be taken with sufficient rise of tide. The next red port hand buoy is Black Jack (*Gp Fl (2) R 4s*) but this is near the NE edge of Calshot Spit so it should either be passed on the correct side or left very close to starboard. Beyond this buoy the water deepens and course may be laid to leave Calshot Castle jetty to port or to cross over to the east side of Southampton Water either to proceed to Hamble or up to Southampton.

On the SE side the Western Approach is marked by the West Bramble (*V Qk Fl (9) 10s*), Thorn Knoll (*Fl G 5s*), North Thorn (*Qk Fl G*) and Calshot (*V Qk Fl*) buoys. On this side also, yachts can avoid the fairway by going on the wrong side of these buoys, and leaving to starboard the yellow Spanker and the green W Knoll and E Knoll buoys. The Bramble Bank varies from time to time in position and depth and is composed of shingle. There is an orange Radar beacon about 1 cable SE of the worst part, which at present dries about 5 ft (1·5 m) at CD. There is also the East Knoll shoal but this has 1 ft (0·3 m) over it at CD, and lies to the SW of Hill Head buoy. To clear the Brambles on the west side, if bound from Cowes to Southampton, keep west of the line of the Royal Yacht Squadron, the West Knoll green buoy and the lightship, and vice versa.

At night it is simplest to keep in or near to Western Approach channel as it is clearly marked by the light buoys shown on the chart. During fog pilotage is assisted by the bell,

Southampton Water: Soundings in metres. add 0·6 m (1·9 ft) at MLWS, 1·7 m (5·6 ft) at MLWN. Based on surveys with the permission of British Transport Docks Board, Southampton. Approaches based on Chart No. 1905, with the permission of HMS Stationery Office and of the Hydrographer of the Navy.

7.2 Calshot Castle and Black Jack

15 sec, on W Bramble, the Horn (2) on Calshot light-vessel and the bell, *30 sec*, on Calshot N Car Buoy.

From the east the approach is equally easy. The channel lies between the land with its offlying shoals on the starboard hand and the buoys on the east side of the Brambles: E Bramble (*V Qk Fl (3) 5s*), Hill Head (*Fl R 2·5s*). Yachts can pass nearly ¼ mile eastward of the Calshot buoy (*V Qk Fl*) and *Bell 30s*, in 15 ft (4·6 m) and shallow draft craft will find nearly 1½ fathoms (2·7 m) nearly a mile to the eastward, but must stand away from the shore when Calshot Spit Lightship bears west as the mud flats on the east side extend a long way off the land. The Coronation Y conical buoy (*Fl Y 5s*) is starboard hand but may be left a cable to port. The small G conical Bald Head starboard hand buoy is moored close to the drying shoal extending off the shore.

The Main Channel

Southampton Water main shipping channel is marked on the port hand (west side) by red can buoys exhibiting *red occulting* or *red flashing lights*: there are also lights at either end of Fawley jetty (*2FR vert*). The starboard (east side) is marked by conical green buoys showing green flashing lights. In addition there are occasional R (port) and G (starboard) buoys nearer the edge of the mud for the use of ships of less draft. The channel itself is clear and wide and the general direction up to the Dockhead is about NW Mag.

On the west side of Southampton Water, after passing Calshot Castle the Esso Refinery jetties are the first conspicuous features, and extend a long way from the shore, on which large oil reservoirs will be seen. At night the whole area is illuminated by the lights and the glare of the excess gas flare stacks reflected in the clouds. For the next 2 miles

7.3. The Hook buoy which is the first starboard hand mark of the big ship channel after Calshot.

beyond the refineries the west shore possesses no particular features except for the measured distance beacons with white triangles situated high on the mud flats. Three red buoys are passed and westward of the third is the Admiralty jetty (*2 FG*), for the old Coastal Forces Base off which there are many large mooring buoys. The Hythe Sailing Club is on the shore just south of it. Hythe ferry pier is ½ mile beyond the Admiralty jetty and once past this the deep channel lies on the east side near the docks.

The starboard hand (east) of Southampton Water is equally clearly marked. Once inside Calshot, after passing the Reach buoy, (*Gp Fl (3) G 10s*), the first buoy on the starboard hand is the Hook (green pillar, *Qk Fl G* and *bell*) but this lies on the edge of the big ship fairway, and from a yachtsman's point of view may almost be considered as placed in mid-channel. Half a mile east of the Hook is the Coronation buoy, previously mentioned. Hamble Point S Car YB buoy (*Qk Fl (6) + L Fl 15s*) is 1 mile farther up, which marks the port side of the entrance to Hamble River, but is a starboard buoy when proceeding up Southampton Water. On Hamble Point will be seen the Fairey Marine works, and about a mile farther up will be seen a number of oil storage tanks and the Shell Mex Jetty. To the north of this is Hawker Siddeley Aviation Ltd, off which there are transit beacons which govern the controlled anchorage for ships of over 300 ft. Hamble Spit which dries out at CD, projects into Southampton Water approximately to a line from Hamble Point Buoy to the end of the Shell Mex Jetty and should be left well to starboard, although in summer months it is marked by the yellow Cathead racing buoy.

Following up the line of the coast for another 2 miles, the site of the Royal Victoria Hospital at Netley, of which only the central dome remains, is brought abeam. From the transit beacons south of the hospital northward to Weston Shelf at the entrance of the River Itchen there is a Hovercraft testing area extending from shallow water approximately to the 2-fathom line. Above Netley the mud runs out a greater distance from the shore and Weston Shelf dries out at CD; at low water even a yacht of light draught will have to keep near to the buoyed channel.

At the Dockhead, which is conspicuous in the middle of Southampton Water, the channel divides, the River Test continuing in a NW direction and the River Itchen branching away to the NNE. Both rivers are referred to under separate headings.

Fawley Basin. The entrance to the 12 ft (3·6 m) dredged channel, leading to the Fawley Power Station, lies $\frac{1}{4}$ mile beyond Calshot Castle on the west side of Southampton Water. It is very clearly marked by pile beacons, with occasional lights at night when in use by ships. There are moorings for local yachts, belonging to members of the Fawley Power Station Social and Sports Club, on the south side between No 10 beacon and the entrance channel and water intake of the Power Station. Across this entrance there is a floating oil boom, the apex of which is secured by anchors with buoys, which are sometimes mistaken by strangers for mooring buoys. Yachts must keep clear of the boom, as there is an undercurrent into the channel. It may be possible on application to obtain the use of a vacant mooring or to anchor close to the port hand beacons temporarily but the

7.4. The Fawley oil terminals on the west side of Southampton Water, opposite to the Hamble River.

slope of the mud is very steep. Visiting yachts must on no account obstruct ships using the dredged channel to the Power Station, and enquiry should be made about their movements. The public landing on the south side of the entrance channel has been reinstated.

Ashlett Creek. The entrance to this creek is just over $\frac{1}{2}$ mile above Fawley Basin and is close to the Fawley R buoy which lies a cable south of the southern end of the Esso jetties. The creek appears to be $\frac{1}{2}$ cable wide at high water but most of it is very shallow, drying up to 8 ft (2·4 m) near Ashlett, except for a very narrow channel which is little more than a gutter winding through the mud. Never-the-less, it provides interesting water for centre-board and light draft craft. The active Esso Sailing Club has a club house near the head of the creek; it is the authority that maintains the navigation and (seasonal) racing marks in the creek.

Keel yachts can use the channel with sufficient rise of tide, but 4 ft (1·2 m) draft is about the maximum without local knowledge, as the channel is difficult to follow at HW springs when the marshes are covered. At low water, keel yachts must sit in mud or dry out alongside the quay.

When entering, leave Fawley buoy (which is in shallow water) close to port and come on to a course of approx 254°. The leading marks that used to give this transit are much decayed, difficult to find and are not being replaced. Ahead should be seen the first of three small R can buoys. At times there is also a spherical Y racing mark (seasonal and not shown on the chartlet) marked ASHLETT, moored on the starboard side of the channel. Follow the three R port hand buoys round the first 90° bend into the SE reach, then round the G starboard hand buoy at the second 90° bend into a long reach to the SW. The channel is very narrow at this bend and one should keep close to the buoy. This next leg of the channel is nearly straight; leading marks are the electricity pole (*RW hor*) near the Sailing Club and the chimney of the red brick cottage with slate roof behind the quay. There are some posts and withies remaining and some with top-marks (G triangles to starboard: R squares to port) but these are placed well up on the mud.

The third 90° bend is to NW, the channel being close to the stern moorings of the boats at the SW bank. Keep well clear of the speed limit Notice Board as there is a short gravel spit running SW of it. Pass close to the post with R square top-mark, which is just north of the end of the public landing stage steps. The channel curves slightly in a thin 'S' bend to a sharp hairpin bend round a post with R square top-mark which leave close to port. After rounding this, head straight back towards the Club flagstaff, then follow the line of moorings to starboard, leaving the SLIP buoy (R) to port. Visiting yachts should now head for the public quay at the head of creek, with moorings to starboard and mud berths to port.

There is also a South Channel, along the line of the Outfall marked by Y beacons, south of the main creek, but this should not be attempted without local knowledge.

Note that old mooring chains cross the creek in a SE direction close to the starboard buoy at the first bend near the entrance and east to west at the second bend.

Ashlett is pretty and consists of a quay and hard, a few houses, the old mill and 'The Jolly Sailor's inn. Yachts can berth at the quay which dries 7 ft (2·1 m) CD, and which is suitable for a scrub. Launching site at hard. Water at the Inn, stores at Fawley, ½ mile distant.

Moorings and Anchorages

Anchorage is possible in Southampton water anywhere clear of the ship fairways and moorings and outside the prohibited areas. Anchorage should be sought under a

7.5. Ashlett Mill and the Quay against which yachts can dry out at low water.

weather shore, according to the wind, and it is wise to buoy the anchor to avoid foul mooring chains or foul bottom. Swell is caused by passing ships. The following are the places most commonly used:

1. *Hamble River*. See Chapter 8.
2. *Off Royal Pier*. There are Docks Board moorings for large yachts.
3. *Netley*. Half a mile north of Netley Dome, there is a good hard with the Netley Abbey Boat Yard adjacent to it. Stores at Netley ¼ mile and bus service. Moorings for small local yachts. The anchorage lies outside these on a lee shore in westerly winds.
4. *Hythe*. Between the line of Hythe Pier and the Admiralty Jetty there is only from 1 to 3 ft (0·3 to 0·9 m) CD. Farther out from the shore there is 5 to 6 ft (1·5 to 1·8 m). The anchorage is reasonable in westerly winds but take care to anchor clear of moorings. Landing is at Hythe pierhead, from which ferries run to Southampton and an electric train to the shore. Marine Services Ltd yacht yard is at the inner end of the pier and has moorings and a service launch. The Hythe Sailing Club is at the shore end of the

Admiralty Jetty, to the south of which the Club has many small moorings. In Hythe itself there is an hotel, shops and facilities of a small town. EC Wednesday.

5. *Rivers Test and Itchen.* See below.

Facilities

Southampton is the administrative centre for the Solent, and has the Weather Centre, Tel: Southampton 28844. Recorded weather forecasts for the coastal area between Poole Harbour and Chichester can be had from Tel: Southampton 8091. There are good facilities for yachts. F. Smith & Son are official agents for charts of which they keep a wide stock, besides nautical instruments and books. They are also compass adjusters. Tillings supply yacht chandlery, as also the yacht yards. Water at Town Quay, Royal Pier or yacht yards. Shops of all kinds. Many of the large shops close all day Mondays, but most of them have early closing on Wednesday. Several hotels and restaurants. Excellent railway services, buses to all parts of Hampshire and motor coaches to London and elsewhere. Red Funnel steamer and hydrofoil service and Hovercraft to Cowes.

RIVERS TEST AND ITCHEN

The River Test. Leaving the Dockhead to starboard and proceeding up the River Test in a NW direction, the Queen Elizabeth II Terminal and the Ocean Dock will be passed. The deep channel lies on the Docks side of the river, whereas beyond the port hand red buoys there is the Gymp shoal and foul ground.

Continuing up the river the Town Quay and Royal Pier will lie to starboard and half-a-mile farther up, the river is divided into two parts, leaving a narrow shoal between

7.6. The southerly point of Southampton Docks. River Test to port and River Itchen to starboard.

the two. The northern is the deep dredged channel running past the Western Docks used by the P & O, Union Castle and other liners, at the end of which is the King George V graving dock and the new container berths. The southern side is the Marchwood Channel, and leads up past Cracknore Hard, Husband's jetty and SW to Marchwood Basin.

To follow the southern part of the river, alter course off the Royal Pier and steer towards No 2 Swinging Ground buoy (red can). Just short of this the yacht will come on to the leading marks for the dredged Marchwood Channel. These are two beacons, the first with a triangle topmark and the second with a diamond topmark. Keeping these in transit at 297°, a Y can buoy (marking the NE corner of the basin dredged to Marchwood Power Station quay) will be left to port and a beacon with a square topmark to starboard. The latter stands in the middle of the shoal between the Marchwood Channel and the northern channel along the docks.

The dredged area of the Marchwood Channel, which leads only to the entrance of Marchwood Basin, ends about ½ cable east of the first beacon with triangle top. Here treat the two beacons as starboard hand marks, passing close to them sailing through the area of the Marchwood SC moorings where the shallowest lie in 1 ft (0·3 m) CD. Well to starboard will be left No 4 and No 6 red Swinging Ground buoys, which are on the north side of the middle ground.

After passing the second beacon bear to port, leaving to port No 8 Swinging Ground buoy (red), to enter the dredged channel for the new container berths.

Alternatively, instead of following the Marchwood Channel, the northern deep ship channel can be used, finally shaping a course leaving No 8 Swinging Ground buoy to port and entering the dredged channel.

Since the Eigth Edition was published, the container berths have been extended and a great area of land reclaimed. South of this the channel has been dredged and is both deep and well marked. Then follow up the river channel, marked by beacons, until arriving at a S. Car YB beacon topped by two cones which marks the junction of two channels.

7·7. The leading line beacons for Marchwood channel.

The northern arm, which is the Test River, leads to Redbridge wharfs. It is marked by appropriate beacons, but it dries out and is of little interest except for centreboard sailing. The western arm leads to Eling where shoal draft yachts can dry out on the mud. Leave the junction beacon and also the five beacons with triangle topmarks to starboard. The channel is extremely narrow and dries 2 ft (0·6 m) at CD close to banks which dry 7 ft (2·1 m). Just short of Eling, after passing under power cables, it turns sharply to the SW into the basin where the best water is on the starboard side. In the middle of the basin is a mud bank, between the shallow gutters of water on the north and south sides. Strangers may find the north side easier, passing the big quay and bringing up at or before the small quay, alongside which there is about 6 ft (1·8 m) at HW springs. Local advice is needed if wishing to remain at low water as the basin is crowded by light draft yachts and small craft. Shops in the built-up area on the north side. EC Wednesday. Launching site at hard on north side. Eling Sailing Club has a landing pontoon, winter quarters and scrubbing hard for its members.

The R Corps of Transport Depot and the R Engineer YC have moorings for their member's yachts downstream of Husband's Shipyard and Marchwood YC has the moorings in the area south of the transit beacons for the Marchwood Channel. The latter has its club house and a slip at the hard beyond Marchwood Power Station. Enquiries about the possibility of temporary vacant moorings may be made at Husband's shipyard or the club. The shipyard is principally commercial, but also undertakes yacht repairs, especially of large yachts. The yard (whose directors are sailing men) supplies fuel and water and has a ferry launch to Southampton Town Quay. The Ship Inn at Cracknore Hard is adjacent but no other facilities are close at hand.

The River Itchen. This river is commercialized and little used by visiting yachts never-the-less Kemp's Yacht Terminal provides convenient mooring facilities for yachtsmen visiting Southampton or, indeed, going to London.

The entrance lies on the east side of the Dockhead between the docks and the mud flats on the starboard hand marked by Weston Shelf conical green buoy (*Gp Fl (3) G 15s*), No 1 Swinging Ground green buoy (*Occ G 4s*) and two dolphins No 1 (*Qk Fl G*) and No 2 (*Fl G 5s*) and the Weston jetty (*2 FG vert*), beyond which is No 3 dolphin (*Fl G 7s*) and No 4 (*Qk Fl G*), while to port there is the Bank beacon *Qk Fl R*. Caution—Continental Ferry Services operate to and from Princess Alexandra's Dock.

About a mile from the entrance, the Itchen bridge (24.4 m) crosses the river. The river then bears NW—and is marked on the port hand by Crosshouse beacon (*Occ R 5 sec*) and a little farther up by Chapel beacon (*Fl G 3s*) on the starboard hand—above which there are no lights, except at jetties and at the Northam Bridge.

For the next ¼ mile above the latter beacon the channel bends to the NE, and the deep water lies on the west side. To starboard the mud extends almost to a line of five mooring buoys. Leaving the last buoy close to starboard, steer off the jetties on the West bank. Here the depth of the channel is 7 ft (2·1 m) but as it is narrow and unmarked in this vicinity it is better to treat it as 5 ft (1·5 m). There is then a semi-circular bend right round to the west which is marked by beacons. Pontoons will be left to starboard before arriving off Kemp's Yacht Terminal which is also left to starboard. Beyond this the river leads east for 3 cables to Northam Bridge and the channel lies on the south side with a very wide expanse of mud on the north. Beyond the road bridge the Itchen is only 2 or 3 ft (0·6 to 0·9 m) deep and not marked, but there are two yards: the Rampart Boatyard and the Belsize Boatyard.

7.8. Kemp's yacht terminal.

There is little room for anchorage out of the fairway in the Itchen river, and most of the moorings are intended for large vessels. Enquiry can be made at the yacht yards and there are berths alongside floating pontoons with walk-ashore landing at Kemp's Yacht Terminal. There is a launching site here and at hards at Southampton and Woolston adjoining the floating bridge. All facilities at Southampton. Banks and small shops also at Woolston. Two sailing clubs, Southampton SC on the east side of River Itchen entrance and Weston SC $\frac{1}{2}$ mile further east.

8 Hamble River & Titchfield Haven

Double High Water: Springs −0 h 25 m and +1 h 35 m Portsmouth; Neaps mean +0 h 20 m. At springs after about 3 hours flood there is a stand for 1½ hours, followed by a 3½ hours rise. The ebb runs strongly for 3½ hours attaining maximum rate 2 hours after second HW.
Tidal Heights above datum at Calshot Castle: MHWS 14·5 ft (4·4 m) MLWS 2·1 ft (0·6 m) MHWN 12 ft (3·6 m) MLWN 6 ft (1·8 m)
Stream sets in the Solent west about −1 h 0 m Portsmouth and east shortly after +4 h 0 m. Note an early stream sets SE at about +3 h 0 m. Portsmouth on the east side of the entrance to Southampton Water opposite Calshot LV when the main Solent stream is still running west.
Depths above datum: For the average yacht of 6 ft (1·8 m) draft the Hamble River is deep, but in reality the bottom is very uneven, much of it being 2 fathoms (3·6 m) and more, with shoal patches such as in the vicinity of the Spit Pile 5 ft (1·5 m) at CD and only 8 ft (2·4 m) off the School of Navigation pier. For this reason it is best to take the depth as 7 ft (2·1 m) which gives about 9 ft (2·7 m) at MLWS up to Badnam Creek. Above this there is something in the nature of a bar with only 5 ft (1·5 m), after which the depths are 6 to 7 ft (1·8 to 2·1 m) up to Bursledon Bridge.
Yacht Clubs: R Southern YC, R Thames YC, R Air Force YC, Household Division YC, Hamble River SC, Warsash SC.

For a considerable time the Hamble River has been one of the largest concentrated yachting centres in the British Isles. Developments continue at what can only be described as a fantastic rate, and the river is packed with yachts the whole 2½ miles from Faireys near the entrance up to Bursledon Bridge. In addition to rows of pile moorings, there are four large well managed and well equipped marinas. What is so interesting is the extraordinary variety of yachts in the river. There are many famous ocean racers and new yachts of every kind to the latest designs, both sail and power, besides great numbers of first rate cruising yachts. Smaller standard types can be counted by the hundred and the picture is broadened by old-timers and other yachts of individual character.

Historically, the river, in common with other Solent harbours, has been the scene of many attacks by invaders from the sea. Cedric and Cynric are said to have landed in the year 519—the year in which the final defeat of the Britons took place. It is certain that it was much attacked in later years by the Danes. Swanwick is one of the place-names in Hampshire which are probably of Danish origin—perhaps originally Sweinwyk.

The river is now controlled by a more orthodox body, the Hampshire County Council, who charge relatively lower dues than were extracted by the Danes. They are actively continuing the developments in the river started by the former Southampton Harbour Board and British Transport Dock Board, Southampton, and some of the pending improvements are referred to below. The former bye-laws still apply. Motor yachts and yachts under auxiliary power must keep to starboard side of the fairway and navigate with care and at a speed such as will not cause damage or danger. Speeds should certainly be low, otherwise the wash causes the utmost inconvenience to those aboard the hundreds of yachts on moorings and can be a danger to children in boats.

Hamble River and Titchfield Haven

8.1. Hamble Point buoy.

The Approach and Channel

The sailing directions for Southampton Water will bring a yacht inside Calshot Castle, when course should be shaped for the Hook green pillar buoy (*Qk Fl G*), which lies in the centre of Southampton Water about $\frac{1}{4}$ mile NE of Calshot Castle. From this point Hamble Point Buoy is situated N by W only $\frac{3}{4}$ mile distant. When approaching from the east, the Hook will be left to the westward, and the course will set to leave the Coronation Buoy (*Y Fl Y 5s*) to starboard, or not more than a cable to port as it is not far off the shoal on the east side of Southampton Water. The unlit Baldhead Buoy (G) must be left to starboard.

When Hamble Point S Car buoy (*Qk Fl (6) + L Fl 15s*) is brought abeam a series of piles marking the channel will be seen. These make the channel clear, but if a transit is desired it will be a red diamond day mark on Pile No. 6 beacon on the port side of the channel in line 345° with a red triangle day mark on a white pole beacon on Hamble common. The port hand piles are fluorescent red with can tops and are marked with even numbers 2, 4, 6, 8 and 10, re-numbered since the 8th Ed. No 2 is now Spit Pile. Do not bring these port hand marks too close aboard. The starboard hand piles are green with green triangular topmarks. They bear odd numbers from 1 to 9, and also should not be approached closely.

The channel bends towards the NE at No 6 pile and the inner entrance to the river is between the Fairey Marine works on the port hand and the end of the College of Nautical Studies (ex School of Navigation) pier on the starboard hand. Here the fairway is on the starboard side of the river. Once inside the river there are fewer navigation marks, but the channel is fairly obvious as there are numbers of yachts moored on both sides of the fairway.

The village of Warsash lies to starboard, where will be seen the prominent black and white Harbourmaster's office building and his pier. Opposite Warsash there is the Hamble Point Marina. A ferry service, dating from some 500 years, still operates between Warsash and Hamble. Hamble itself is about $\frac{1}{2}$ mile farther up the river on the port hand. The Southern YC, RAFYC and Port Hamble Marina will be seen.

8.2. The inner entrance of the river with Fairey Marine on the port side. The yacht on the right is in the fairway.

The bends in the river are shown on the chart. As the first bend to the NNW is approached about $\frac{1}{4}$ mile above the Hamble Marina there was an isolated gravel bank. Many yachts used to run aground on this but it is now west of the port hand piles. On the port hand just before the next Badnam Creek, where yachtsmen will find the Mercury Yacht Harbour, and beyond it lies the extensive Lincegrove Marsh, which is broken up into many small shallow creeks, and is marked by a white beacon. On the opposite side of the river is a beacon and tide gauge marking the edge of the extensive mud flats on the starboard hand. The river then takes a NE direction to Swanwick and the fairway lies between mooring piles on either hand.

8.3. Warsash and the Harbour Master's modern office building and his pier in the foreground.

At the end of this reach is a sharp turn from NE to NW and a stranger approaching the bend will see yachts apparently lying to piles in the middle of the river and more yachts not far from them lying on moorings on the east side. This is because there is a mud shoal at the bend on the port side extending almost halfway across the river, which is marked by a red beacon. This must be left to port as also the line of mooring piles beyond it but the yachts on moorings are left to starboard.

8.4. The sharp bend at Swanwick shore leading to Moody's yard and marina. Near LW keep further to starboard.

Above Swanwick there are two short reaches; first, north-west to Bursledon leaving Moody's pier and large marina to starboard and then north-east up to the bridge. The deep channel is much narrower in these upper reaches and lies close to the piles on the port hand. The wind is fickle when it is blowing off the high ground on the west side. There is a shoal on the starboard side of the channel close above Moody's Swanwick Marina.

Beyond Bursledon Bridge there is a railway bridge and a motor-way bridge. In the reach between them there are houseboats and motor yachts lying on moorings. At high water the channel is navigable in a dinghy or by light draft craft as far as Botley, about 3 miles above the bridge; in fact, the channel is fairly wide and over a fathom deep for much of the distance. The river runs between densely wooded shores and is very pretty.

Lights: Leading lights are established which lead up the outer two reaches of the river channel as far as Warsash. The first pair consist of the light *Gp Occ (2) R 12 sec* on

No 6 Pile beacon in line at 345° with a rear beacon *Qk Fl red* on Hamble Common, which has an arc of 8°. The lights for the next transit up to Warsash are a light *Qk Fl G* on the Warsash Shore Beacon on the drying line on the starboard hand between the College of Nautical Studies pier and the Warsash SC jetty (ex RTYC) and a light *Iso G 6s* over an arc of 8 ° on the rear beacon mounted on the Rising Sun Hotel, the transit being 024°. This will lead to a position abreast the College pier ((*2 FR vert*). Beyond this, the river is marked as

8.5. The Royal Southern Yacht Club in Hamble village with its floating dinghy pontoon.

far as Bursledon Point beacon by six quick flashing red lights on piles on the port hand and seven quick flashing green lights on the starboard hand.

Moorings, Anchorage and Facilities

There is no room left in the Hamble River for anchoring, except in between No 6 port hand pile and No 9 Starboard pile, clear of the landing transit. Here it is rough in fresh SW winds and during daytime it is disturbed by the wakes of constantly passing motor yachts, so it is useful only if arriving at night waiting for daylight to continue up the river.

The Harbour Master (Capt A. C. D. Leach, DSC VRD) and his Assistant (Mr K. V. G. Willis) have an office and jetty at Warsash shore, Tel: Locks Heath 6387. The Administrative Officer (Mr E. J. Sainsbury) mans the office during office hours. Application should be made to the Harbour Master for berthing, but the following positions are available for visiting yachts and bear notices to this effect.

Warsash. Piles on the port hand of the main fairway Nos B1 to 4.

Hamble. Opposite Port Hamble piles on the starboard side Nos 9 to 16.

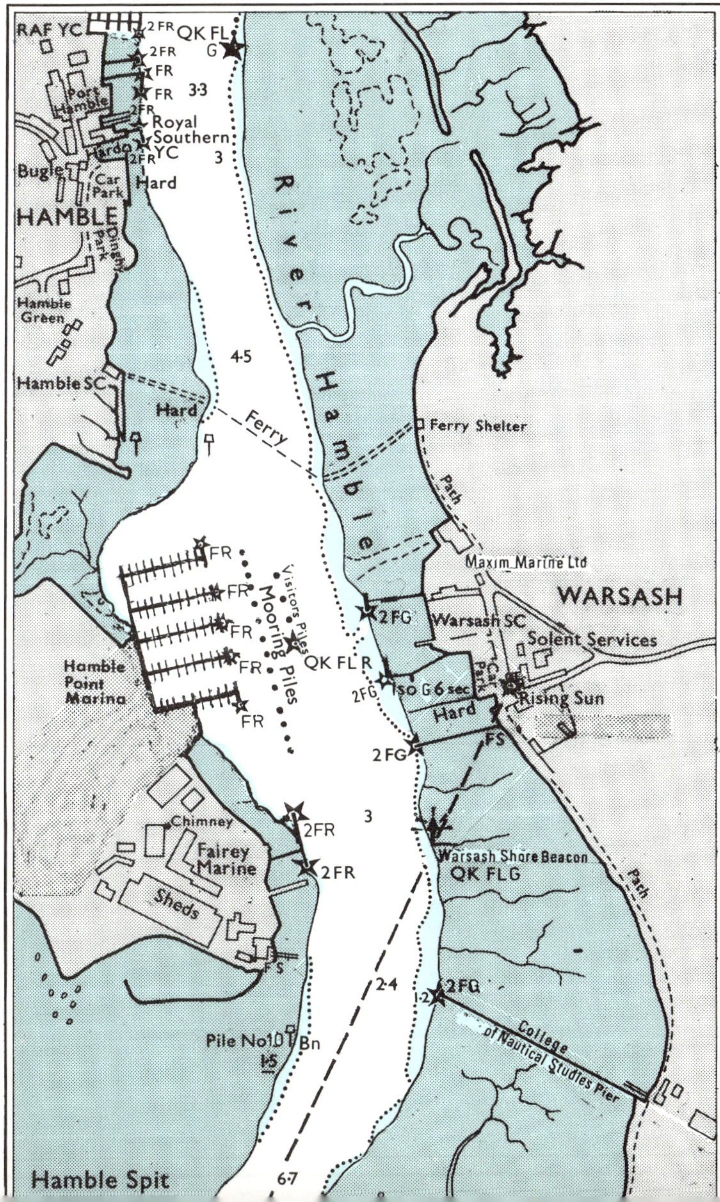
RAF YC
QK FL G
2FR
FR
3·3
Port Hamble
Royal Southern YC
Hardo
3
Bugle
Car Park
Hard
HAMBLE
Dinghy Park
Hamble Green
4·5
Hamble SC
Hard
Ferry
River Hamble
Ferry Shelter
Path
Maxim Marine Ltd
WARSASH
Warsash SC
Solent Services
Visitors Piles
Mooring Piles
QK FL R
Iso G 6 sec
Rising Sun
Car Park
Hard
2FG
FS
Hamble Point Marina
Chimney
Fairey Marine
Sheds
Warsash Shore Beacon
QK FLG
2·4
1·2
Pile No1
Bn
1·5
College of Nautical Studies Pier
Hamble Spit
6·7
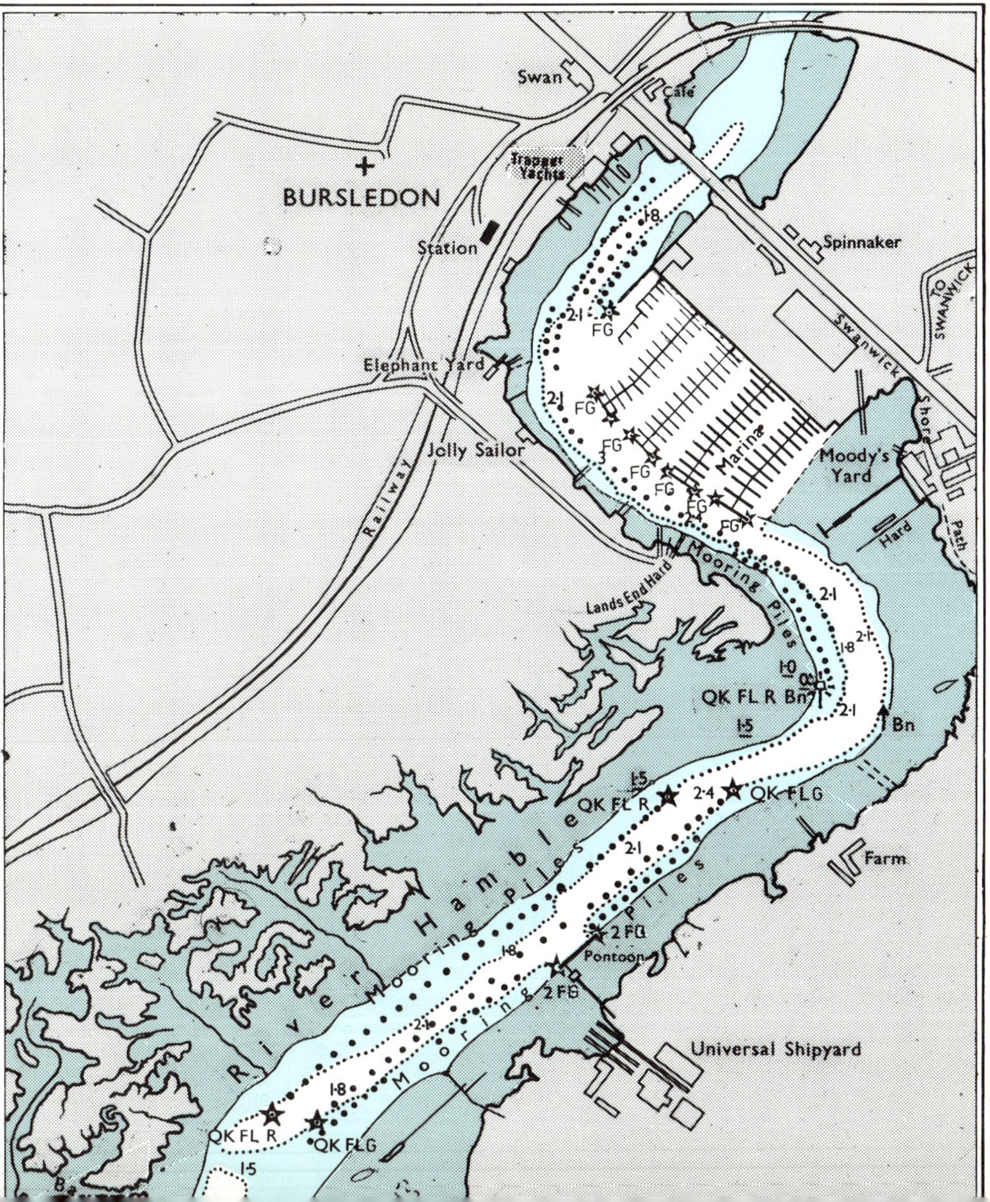
Swan
Cafe
BURSLEDON
Trapper Yachts
Station
Spinnaker
TO SWANWICK
Swanwick Shore
Elephant Yard
Jolly Sailor
Railway
FG
2·1
1·8
Marina
Moody's Yard
Hard
Path
Lands End Hard
Mooring Piles
1·0
QK FL R Bn
1·5
Bn
QK FL R
QK FLG
2·4
Farm
River Hamble
Mooring Piles
2FG
Pontoon
Universal Shipyard

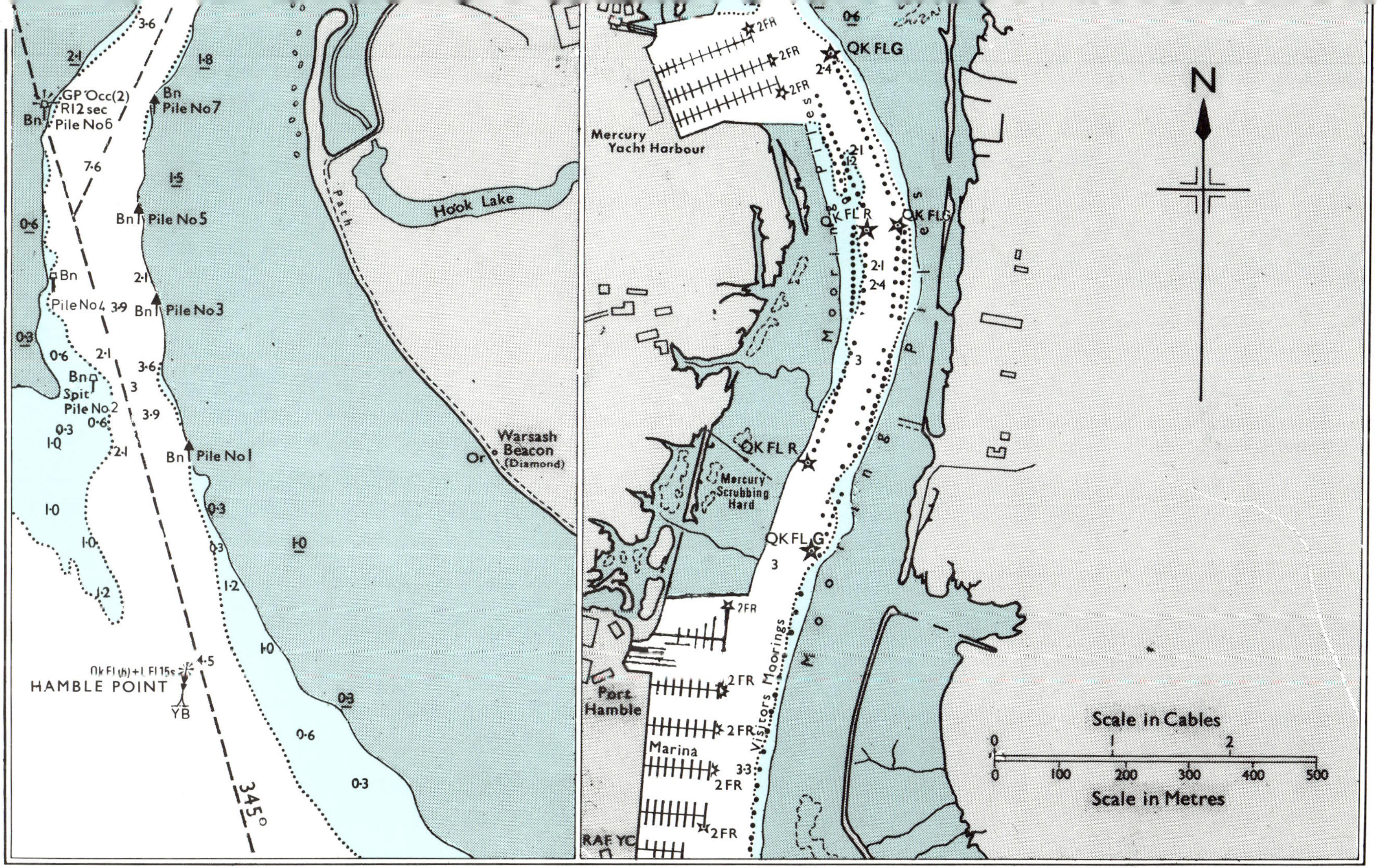

Hamble River: Soundings in metres. Add 0·6 m (2·1 ft) at MLWS, 1·8 m (6·0 ft) at MLWN. Based on surveys with the permission of British Transport Docks Board, Southampton and Hampshire County Council.

Hamble River and Titchfield Haven

There are three public scrubbing hards. The Warsash Hard just off The Rising Sun Hotel; the Mercury Scrubbing Hard, where one is advised to berth N of the pile; and the Lands End Hard opposite Swanwick Marina. All three are operated on a first-come-first-served basis and free of charge for the first 48 hours.

Berths may also be available on application at Port Hamble and Swanwick marinas, as also at the Mercury Yacht Harbour and Hamble Point Marina. It is wise to book in advance. The yacht yards may also be able to advise on moorings temporarily available in the absence of their owners, and the yacht clubs have moorings which if temporarily vacant may be available, on application, to members of affiliated clubs or other approved visitors.

Water and fuel may be had at any of the yacht marinas or yacht yards. Customs' launches for clearance. The Customs' office is at Port Hamble Ltd, Tel: Hamble 2007 and arrangements may be made there for bonded stores from Southampton.

8.6. The fuelling berth of the Port Hamble Marina which is just above the Royal Southern Yacht Club on the port hand.

At Warsash there is the Maxim Marine Ltd fully equipped yacht yard and chandlery and nearby is the 'Rising Sun' hotel and the Solent School of Yachting. There is a car park and hard suitable for launching. Restaurants include Edwardo's, Cortigo (formerly the 'Crab and Lobster') and 'Le Bon Viveur'. A quarter mile up the main road there is the yacht equipment works of M. S. Gibb, a PO, banks and several small shops. EC Thursday. Buses to Gosport, Bursledon and Southampton.

At Hamble there is the large marina of Port Hamble, operated by Rank Marine International Ltd with the usual marina facilities, including fuel. The yard here is operated by Fairways Marine Ltd. J. R. Williams (Chandlery) Ltd at Hamble make and repair sails as also Lucas and Davies. Launching sites at the public hard or Port Hamble. There are other chandlers, yacht agents, three banks and shops of most kinds in the village. EC Wednesday. Restaurants: Bugle Inn, Atlantic Restaurant, The Wheelhouse café and Hamble Manor Hotel. Buses to Woolston, Bursledon and Southampton. The R Southern YC is close to the hard. South of this is a car park (and another is in the village) and the dinghy enclosure. The RAF YC just south of Port Hamble Ltd at the end of the Ropewalk, and Hamble River SC by the ferry hard.

Farther up the river at Badnam Creek on the west side $\frac{3}{4}$ mile (1·2 km) from Hamble is the Mercury Yacht Harbour, also operated by Rank Marine International. There are the usual marina arrangements for water and electricity, but for repairs, laying-up, other yard work and for fuel, yachts are taken to Port Hamble. In the next reach there is the jetty (with fuel and water) of Universal Shipyards Ltd. At Swanwick Shore, farther up the river where it bends to NW is a public hard (launching site), the jetty and dinghy landing pontoon of A. H. Moody and Son Ltd.

At this old established family yard with a new look, there is every conceivable requirement, including yacht agency and chandlers, for yachts of all sizes. The large Swanwick Marina adjoins the yard and has been considerably extended on the NW end. On the opposite side of the main road is the smaller Profile Marine Ltd, Greenham Marine (electronics) and a garage. Bruce Banks Sails at Sarisbury and Ian Proctor Metal Masts are in easy reach by car or bus. There is a grocer near Moody's and 100 yards up the Swanwick road is another grocer, PO and butcher. Hot and cold snacks at the 'Red Lion' ('regrettably now renamed 'The Spinnaker'), restaurant at the 'Old Ship' (best to book in advance) or across the bridge at the 'Swan'. Buses to Southampton, Fareham, Gosport and Warsash.

The village of Bursledon is a little higher up the river on the west side with landing at the steps by the 'Jolly Sailor' or at the hard by the bridge, but the end of the latter dries out before LW. The Elephant Boat Yard for yachts up to about 10 tons TM is just beyond the 'Jolly Sailor' and near the bridge is the larger Trapper Yachts Ltd with alongside moorings. Adjacent to the yard is the chandlery (J. & G. Meakes) who also supply marine craft, outboards and a range of yacht clothing. Opposite is the Cabin Boatyard, Stores and Restaurant. Foulkes & Son's boatyard is just beyond the railway bridge. Launching site (often congested) at Land's End a cable SE of 'Jolly Sailor', at the bridge hard or by arrangement with Trapper's or at the boatyards above the bridges. Grocers and PO at Old Bursledon. Restaurant at 'Swan Hotel' and up the hill at the 'Crow's Nest'. Station at Bursledon, main road bus stop at 'Swan' and the Hamble bus stop at 'Crow's Nest'.

TITCHFIELD HAVEN

Titchfield Haven lies 3 miles SE of Hamble River and at the west end of Hill Head. This attractive Lilliputian harbour consists of a mud camber at the entrance of the River Meon south of the sluice under the coast road. It is protected from north and west but is very small and dries out at low water springs, so that it is only suitable for centre-board dinghies and very shoal draft yachts, such as twin keelers which can take the bottom. Anchorage outside is possible in offshore winds but it will be far from the haven, as the sand and shingle dries out $\frac{1}{4}$ mile at LW springs, so that even entering it by dinghy involves a wait for sufficient rise of tide (allowing for drying 5 to 7 ft (1·5 to 2·1 m) at CD, except when sufficient river water is coming down.

Titchfield Haven

The Camber lies behind a shingle spit to the west of which is the coastal road above the sea wall, parking space and further west many bathing huts. To the northward of the spit there is a large, white house, a clump of trees just east of it and a large red brick house with other houses still further eastwards. The best approach (which can be made only with sufficient rise of tide over the drying sand and shingle) is with the brick house bearing 020°. This leads about 100 yards ESE of the end of the spit. A small beacon with diamond top-mark (one of the marks for the Hill Head Sailing Club's start line) is in the channel and should be left close to starboard before altering course in a curve to the west almost parallel with the land.

The Hill Head Sailing Club occupies a prominent position on the sea wall just to the east of the entrance. The Club (Tel: Stubbington 4843) or their representative Mr T. Robertson (Tel: Stubbington 2768) who acts as Harbour Master for the Club, should be consulted if wishing to remain and dry out as most of the camber is occupied by private moorings. A visiting yacht could well bring to temporarily near the bridge, but the bottom is foul and old timbers and piles make it a bad spot to dry out. At Hill Head, ½ mile east of the haven, on the bus route, is the 'Osborne View Hotel', garage, shops, PO and the Hill Head Chandlers, Tel: Stubbington 4621).

8.8. Titchfield Haven can only be approached with sufficient rise of tide over the drying sand and shingle. The modern building on the sea wall is the Hill Head SC. Opposite can be seen a small metal beacon, which is in the middle of what channel there is.

8.7. The shallow channel which is formed by the outflow from the River Meon on the right bends almost parallel with the shore and is marked by two perches on the starboard hand. This picture near low water shows where it enters The Camber.

9 Wootton Creek

High Water: Springs mean −0 h 10 m Portsmouth; Neaps +0 h 5 m.
Tidal Heights above datum: MHWS 14·9 ft (4·5 m) MLWS 2·3 ft (0·7 m) MHWN 12·2 ft (3·6 m) MLWN 6 ft (1·7 m).
Stream sets outside to the westward about −1 h 30 m Portsmouth and to the eastward +4 h 20 m.
Depths: Dredged up to 6 ft (1·8 m) CD as far as the ferry terminal but silting occurs. Shallow beyond.
Yacht Club: Royal Victoria Yacht Club.

Wootton is one of the Solent creeks with charm and individuality but unfortunately of recent years there has been considerable silting in the pool which provides the only part where a visiting yacht can remain at low water, unless she is of shoal draft and can lie up the river on the mud. Nevertheless, when there is room the pool can still be used at neap tides by yachts up to 4½ ft (1·4 m) draft or a little more—see below.

Quarr Abbey is situated ½ mile to the eastward. Very little of the old abbey itself remains beyond the ruins of the Abbot's kitchen and fragments of the wall. This was originally built in the reign of Henry I, but the present building was erected less than 100 years ago by Benedictine monks. It is said to be one of the largest buildings built of bricks, and was designed by one of the monks.

9.1. Wootton Beacon.

9.2. The leading mark triangles on the west shore if proceeding up the creek.

The Approach, Entrance and Creek

The entrance to Wootton Creek lies two miles west of Ryde Pier and is clearly marked by Wootton Beacon (*Qk Fl*) and three further beacons on the west side of the channel. No special directions are necessary for the approach from the east, but, as the mud flats run out a long way, the shore must be given a wide berth. Sail from the outer end of Ryde Pier towards Barton Point, which is the point beyond King's Quay, 1½ miles east of Old Castle Point. Then, when Wootton Beacon is seen steer in towards it.

To approach from the west, an imaginary line from Old Castle Point to the shore end of Ryde Pier will clear all dangers handsomely, and as soon as Wootton Bridge village opens up, Wootton rocks (marked by a R buoy) will have been passed.

Having arrived off the beacons, alter course to steer up the straight channel leaving the four beacons close to starboard as the fairway, which is dredged to 6 ft (1·8 m) CD, is very narrow and the flats on its east side are unmarked. There is little room for tacking and the car ferries require most of the fairway, especially at low water, when it is best to wait until the channel is clear of any ferry seen approaching. Although the channel is deep up to the ferry pier, there is no point in entering it until there is sufficient rise of tide to sail up the river or to enter the pool, which now dries at MLWS.

If continuing to the pool, then on arrival at No. 3 Beacon head for the end of the Ferry Pier and leave this 6 ft to port. Once past the end of the pier the yacht will be in the pool where yachts lie at moorings or at anchor.

If wishing to proceed up Wootton Creek instead of to the pool, there is a turn to the

starboard after passing No 3 Beacon. The channel is marked by R (port hand) and G (starboard hand) buoys and by leading marks which can be seen on the shore below the woods to the west. These consist of two white triangles on frames (see photograph).

The best indication of the channel after the leading marks is to follow the line of moored craft leaving them to starboard. The channel is narrow but with a sufficient rise of tide a $3\frac{1}{2}$ ft (1·1 m) draft yacht can get right up to the top of the creek.

Lights: The beacons carry lights Wootton Beacon *Qk Fl*, No 1 *Fl G 3s*, No. 2 *Gp Fl (2) G 5s*, No 3 *Qk Fl G*.

Moorings, Anchorage and Facilities

Wootton Creek comes under the authority of the Queen's Harbour Master at Portsmouth. His authority over the allocation of moorings and navigation in the creek is exercised through a private association, the Wootton Creek Fairways Committee (Hon Sec Mr R. W. Perraton, The Moorings, Sloop Lane, Wootton Bridge). Advice on moorings can best be obtained from the Manageress of the Royal Victoria Yacht Club, Miss M. King (Tel: Wootton Bridge 882325). Yachts must not at any time anchor in the fairway or where the car ferries turn to the hard. The ferries use the channel by day and night. There is no water in the pool at MLWS and it dries out at CD, but the mud is soft and yachts of moderate draft and twin keel craft can take the ground and remain upright.

9.3. The Royal Victoria Yacht Club and slipway.

Except in strong northerly or easterly winds, the pool is a good place in which to bring up. Most of the moorings are for visitors and there are plans for mooring piles as well. The Royal Victoria Yacht Club welcomes visiting yachtsmen. The club has a dinghy hard, car park, changing-rooms and bar. Water, stores, bread, milk etc, can be obtained there and also meals. Nearby at Fishbourne there is a garage, and the Fishbourne Inn, which serves meals. There is a launching site at HW and J. D. Young & Son build dinghies.

In the upper reaches of the creek, the narrow channel is also occupied by moorings, but anchorage is possible on the mud for shoal draft craft, such as twin keelers, which can dry out. At the top of the creek there is a public landing on the west side. This will give access to three small boatyards: McCutcheon's, Fulford's and Sheen's. On the east side of the creek close to the bridge there are marine engineers, Prefabricated Metals. At Wootton Village there are garage, butchers, grocers, PO, bakers. EC Thursday. Good bus service on main road to Ryde and Newport.

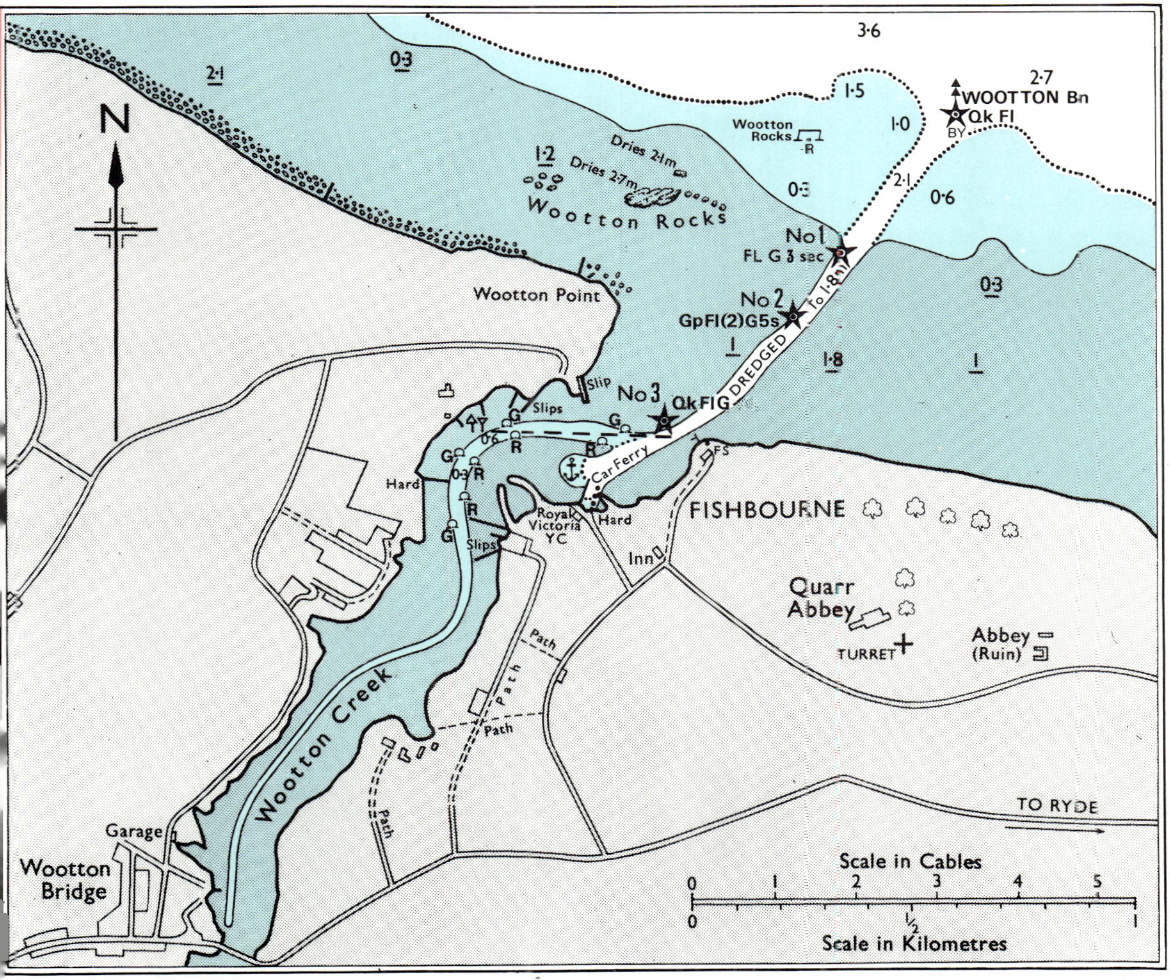

Wootton Creek: Soundings in metres. Add 0·7 m (4·5 ft) at MLWS, 1·8 m (6·0 ft) at MLWN. Based on British Admiralty Chart No. 394, with the permission of HM Stationery Office and of the Hydrographer of the Navy.

Wootton Creek

Anchorage Outside: Temporary anchorage is possible outside in moderate offshore winds, preferably to west of Wootton Bn, and there is a popular anchorage at week-ends further to the west in Osborne Bay. A good position is off the HM Hard, $\frac{1}{2}$ mile west of Barton Point, but this is within the grounds of Osborne House and landing is not permitted. The anchorage (taking soundings to find the right depth) is reasonably sheltered from W and S winds and the stream is weak.

KING'S QUAY CREEK

This shallow trickle of water lies about a mile NW of Wootton, and looks from the sea to be larger than it is in reality. There is no neighbouring village, and the creek is equally difficult to approach either from land or sea, but, nevertheless, is attractive.

Years ago small yachts occasionally entered King's Quay and anchored among the exceptionally beautiful surroundings, but the channel is now unmarked. The creek itself is very narrow and winds between steep mud banks, but is worth exploring on a rising tide in a shallow draft craft or a centreboard dinghy.

At low water there is but a trickle in the "Gutter", as it used to be called. The entrance is difficult to recognise from the north and is to the west of the little marshy valley which the gutter drains. A careful approach to the shore-line on a south westerly course should be made on a rising tide. A small white notice board gives an indication of the best course of approach and, as the shore-line gets near, the channel of the gutter will be seen leading nearly parallel to the shore-line. At high water the marshes are mostly covered, the banks of the gutter will not be seen and entry without prior knowledge very difficult. The gutter winds through the marshes towards the woods, where it takes a sharp turn to the north west coming finally to a pool just below a decayed stone bridge and barrage. In this pool some 4 feet of water remains when the gutter has virtually dried out.

The banks are private property and the bottom of the creek is rented from the Crown by the Nature Conservancy which administers and wardens some 40 acres of the area as a nature reserve. Landing is forbidden and the landing of dogs, in particular, would be very unwelcome.

9.4. The entrance to King's Quay creek. The post on the left marks the end of a mud bank that runs nearly parallel with the shore.

10 Portsmouth Harbour

Tidal Heights above datum: MHWS 15·4 ft (4·7 m) MLWS 2 ft (0·6 m) MHWN 12·5 ft (3·8 m) MLWN 5·8 ft (1·7 m). Flood 7 hours. Ebb 5 hours.
Stream sets to the NW outside at Spithead about −2 h 0 m Portsmouth and to the SE about +3 h 30 m Portsmouth, but the direction of the streams vary in the approach in relation to the local Portsmouth streams.
Depths: Ample at any state of the tide in the main ship channel.
Principal Yacht Clubs: R Albert YC, Royal Naval SA (and Service clubs), Hardway SC, Portsmouth SC, Gosport Cruising Club, Portsmouth Harbour Cruising Club.

Portsmouth has been closely linked with the Navy from the Middle Ages down to the Napoleonic wars and to present times. Nelson's *Victory* is open to visitors in the oldest dry dock in the world, and the frigate *Foudroyant*, built only 12 years after Trafalgar, is moored in the harbour and is reputed to be the oldest ship afloat. Although guided missile ships now replace the frigates of old, Portsmouth Harbour remains predominantly associated with the Royal Navy and comes under the jurisdiction of the Queen's Harbour Master.

The harbour covers an area of some 15 square miles which, apart from the dock area, consists of mud flats intersected by deeper creeks, of which Fareham and Portchester are the principal—*see next chapter*. Increasing use of the harbour has been made by yachtsmen in recent years, with Camper and Nicholson's marina near the entrance and club or private yacht moorings in almost every accessible part where permission has been given to lay them. There is plenty of local racing, and at Southsea the Royal Albert YC provides the starting line for the majority of ocean races and JOG events.

The Approach and Entrance

Straightforward chart work is all that is required for entry to Portsmouth, as the fairway is deep enough for an aircraft carrier and is well marked. Except at LW springs there is also enough water for most yachts on each side of the buoyed channel clear of the big ship fairway.

Approaching from the west it is usually quickest to follow the swashway used by the Portsmouth-Ryde ferries, which leads between the Hamilton Bank on its NW side and the Spit Bank on the SE side. The transit for this swashway is the conspicuous white Naval Memorial on the Southsea shore, about $\frac{1}{4}$ mile east of Clarence Pier, in line with St Jude's Church at 047°. Except at LW springs it is not necessary to adhere exactly to the transit. When No 2 red can buoy is abeam, alter course to port up the fairway to the entrance where a beacon and the Round Tower will be left to starboard and the prominent Fort Blockhouse to port. If desired, follow the transit of Trinity Church,

10.1. Leading marks for swashway between Spit and Hamilton Banks. St. Jude's church spire in line with the war memorial at 047°. Royal Albert YC signal station to left of the memorial.

Gosport, in line with the SW corner of Fort Blockhouse at 313°, altering course for the entrance when the Round Tower on the east side bears north.

Alternatively, with sufficient rise of tide and moderate weather, the inner swashway, which is often used by the Portsmouth-Wootton car ferries, affords a short cut westward of Hamilton Bank in 1 ft (0·3 m) least water. The transit is the west side of a high conspicuous tank in line with the west extremity of Round Tower at 029°. However, there is only a difference of about 2 ft (0·6 m) in being on or off the correct transit. Local yachtsmen often merely follow the Haslar shore, keeping about a cable off it, with sufficient rise of tide, but this is not recommended in strong S to E winds, owing to the cross seas washing back from the sea wall.

From the eastward, vessels proceed off the Horse Sand Fort, up the buoyed channel towards Southsea Castle lighthouse in line with St Jude's Church spire at 003° and then alter course at Castle conical G buoy to follow the fairway to the entrance. If coming from Langstone or Chichester Harbours, distance can be saved by taking the gap in the submerged barrier ¾ mile south of Southsea Beach. *See Chapter 13.*

The flood tide starts at +5 h 30 m Portsmouth and runs easy for 3 hours, and then strong for 4 hours; the ebb starts at +15 m Portsmouth and runs easy for one hour increasing to maximum on the 3rd and 4th hour, attaining 5 knots at springs, and then eases. At the entrance of the harbour, however, owing to the mass of water running out of the creeks, the ebb continues to run hard for longer, and only slackens during the last ¾ hour. Yachtsmen are not advised to attempt entry at the 3rd and 4th hours of the ebb at springs, particularly when strong SE winds against a fast ebb will cause big seas just outside the entrance. When sailing against the stream it should be remembered that there is slacker water on either shore and sometimes a helpful eddy on the east side as far as

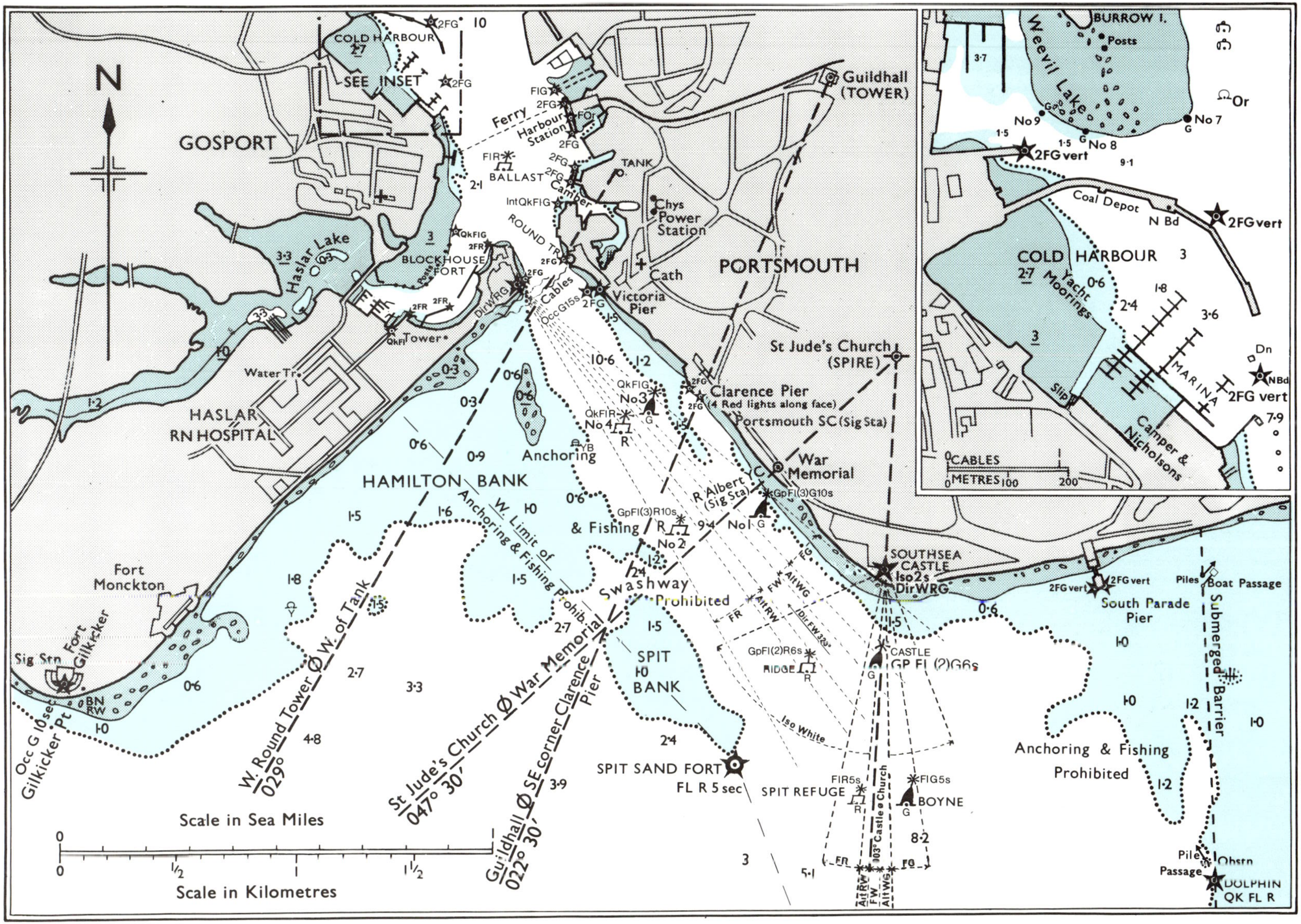

Approaches to Portsmouth Harbour: Soundings in metres. Add 0·6 m (2·0 ft) at MLWS, 1·7 m (5·8 ft) at MLWN. Based on British Admiralty Chart No. 394, with the permission of HM Stationery Office and of the Hydrographer of the Navy.

Portsmouth Harbour

10.2. The leading marks for the inner swashway are the western edge of the conspicuous tank in line with the western extremity of the round tower at 029°.

Round Tower. Caution must be taken to keep out of the way of HM ships, RFA tankers etc, when entering especially under sail in light airs—see signals below:

1. **Day.** Red flag with white diagonal bar.
   Night. Red light over two green lights vertical. No vessel is to leave or enter the Harbour Channel, or approach from seaward N of Outer Spit buoy.
2. **Day.** Red flag with white diagonal bar over one black ball. No vessel is to enter the Harbour Channel from seaward. Outgoing vessels may proceed.
3. **Day.** One black ball over red flag with white diagonal bar. No vessel may leave the harbour, but ingoing vessels may enter.
4. **Day.** Large black pennant.
   Night. White light over two red lights vertical. No vessel is to anchor in the Man-of-War anchorage at Spithead.
5. **Day.** International Code Pendant superior to Pendant zero. HM ship entering, leaving or shifting berth. Keep clear.
6. **Day.** International Code Pendant superior to Pendant nine.
   Night. Three green lights vertical. Warning HM ship under way. All vessels give a wide berth.
7. **Day.** International Code Pendant superior flags NE.
   Night. Green over red light. Proceed with great caution at easy speed. (Signal from Blockhouse Signal Station when ships—other than car ferries—leave the Camber.)
8. **Day.** Flag E.
   Night. Red light, amber light. Submarine entering or leaving Haslar Lake. Light flashes when submarine under way. Keep clear.
9. **Day.** International Code Pendant superior to Flag A.
   Night. Two red lights horizontal. Night, by diving boat all round red light in stern and bows. Have divers down.

Local Sound Signals: *These are not Fog Signals*

Signal	Meaning
–	Am steaming ahead.
– –	Am stopped. Sounded: Power driven vessels in risk of collision.
• • • • •	Am about to turn round to starboard.
• • • • • •	Am about to turn round to port. Sounded: Power driven vessels including a tug with tow.
• • • •	Am unable to keep out of your way. All vessels keep clear.

Should the above signals be observed after the yacht is in the channel, then she should leave or keep to the side of the fairway until the Naval vessel has passed, which can usually be done by yachts with perfect safety. In particular, yachts must keep absolutely clear of large Naval vessels in the narrow harbour entrance between Fort Blockhouse and the Round Tower.

Lights: At night an incoming vessel should keep in the white sector of Southsea Castle light, *Iso 2s Dir WRG*, entering the ship fairway between the Outer Spit S Cardinal buoy *Qk Fl (6) + L Fl 15s* and the starboard hand Horse Sand buoy *Fl G 2·5s*. Thence proceed by chart in the well-marked channel. Fort Blockhouse at the entrance to the harbour has a *Dir WRG light* and incoming vessels should keep in the White sector.

10.3. Entrance to Portsmouth Harbour. Blockhouse Fort to the left. Marina inside the entrance to the left, Round Tower to the right.

Moorings, Anchorage and Facilities

As stated earlier, the Queen's Harbour Master is vested with jurisdiction within Portsmouth Harbour and, indeed, outside from the Needles to the Nab. His office is within the Naval Dockyard, so it is best to contact him by telephone, Portsmouth 22351, ext. 2008, as moorings (other than those allotted to clubs, yacht yards and licence holders) are under his control, which also extends to anchorages.

A visiting yachtsman will have to obtain the use of a mooring or marina berth at least temporarily. If possible a booking should be made in advance, as few anchorages are available owing to prohibited areas, fairways for shipping and cables. The bottom is foul in many parts, so anchors should always have a trip line. The following yacht bases are listed in order of approach:

(a) **Anchorage Outside.** The Royal Albert Yacht Club, Tel: Portsmouth 25924 has a

dinghy slipway and a few moorings off Southsea Beach near the War Memorial and it may be possible to use one if permission is obtained from the club. There is room to anchor, clear of the moorings, but the position is uncomfortable except in offshore winds; there is a swell from passing vessels and it is far from facilities.

(b) **The Camber.** This is the commercial harbour of Portsmouth, situated just within the entrance on the east side. Permission to enter and berth should be obtained from the Harbour Master whose office is at the stone steps at the narrows in the entrance. Tel: Portsmouth 20436/7. The Camber is used by the Isle of Wight car ferries and is usually packed with coasters, lighters and fishing boats, so it is not suitable for visiting yachts

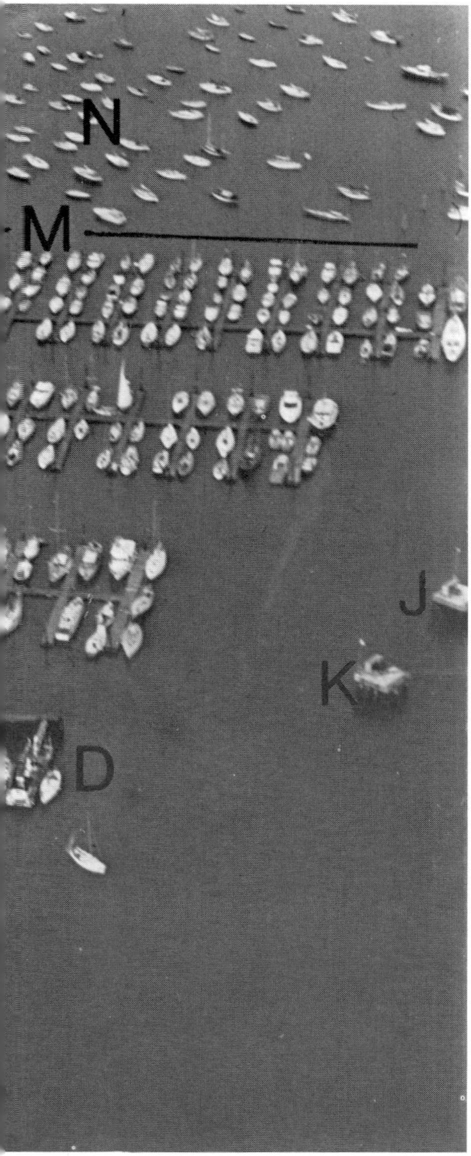

10.4. Camper and Nicholson's marina from the air.

KEY

A Shipyard
B Old Renner Pier
C New Renner Dock
D Fuel Barge
E Pier
F Office
G Car Parks
H Brow
J Naval Mooring Dolphin
K Naval Mooring Dolphin
L Town Quay
M Channel to Town Quay
N Gosport Council Moorings

other than those proceeding to the yacht yards of George Feltham & Sons, Mr Harry Feltham or to the sailmakers and chandlery of Lucas and Son.

(c) **Haslar Lake.** This creek lies on the west side just round Fort Blockhouse. The channel is deep and lies along the SW side between the jetty (where submarines berth) and an extensive mud flat on the NW side, marked by dolphins. It then turns west to Haslar bridge and the depth decreases to 6 ft (1·8 m) CD. Yachts with lowering masts can pass under the bridge into the continuation of the creek which is called Alverstoke Lake. The channel is marked by piles but is very shallow.

The Joint Services Sail Training Centre operates from a complex of pontoons at the south west of Haslar Lake, near Haslar bridge, and there are many Service owned craft moored there. There are also pontoons and moorings on the north west side. There is no specific provision for visiting yachts. Anchorage is limited and the bottom is foul. All facilities at Gosport.

(d) **Gosport.** Camper and Nicholson's have moorings for large yachts off their yard, which is situated a cable above the ferry landing stage at Gosport, and also the big marina which has extensive facilities for yachts of all sizes. The berths here are usually let, but some may be temporarily vacant. Visitors should enquire at the fuel jetty or at the visitors' berths at the end of the third pontoon, but should not enter any other berth until permission has been given by the Berthing Master. Tel: Gosport 80221. Water laid on at pontoons. Fuel at marina jetty. F. Smith and Son for charts, nautical instruments and chandlery by marina offices. Yacht building, repairs and laying up at Camper and Nicholsons.

Beyond Camper and Nicholson's marina lies the Gosport Borough Yacht Harbour in the Cold Harbour. Both marinas are largely enclosed by a long, open-piled oil fuel jetty used by naval tankers. The Gosport Borough Yacht Harbour contains sets of double moorings, let on a long-term basis, but visitors are accommodated if there are temporary vacancies. Application should be made at the blue hut on the quay. Tel: Gosport 83482. Vessels may also make fast alongside the Town Quay, but this dries out and is never very pleasant. The adjacent scrubbing piles on the hard may be used on application.

Besides the facilities already mentioned, there are shops of all kinds in the town including yacht chandlers (EC Wednesday Gosport and Portsmouth; Thursday Southsea) and also small restaurants and many pubs. Ferries to Portsmouth and buses to all parts. Landing steps (drying) near the ferry, and public launching site at Gosport Borough Yacht Harbour.

(e) **Weevil Lake and Forton Lake.** All available space in Weevil Lake is occupied by permanent moorings. The entrance lies north of the Cold Harbour immediately beyond the long jetty. This is left to port and a mud bank marked by piles lies on the starboard hand. The channel then turns sharply northward passing behind Burrow Island before bending to the west, where a wooden foot bridge separates it from Forton Lake. Depths in Weevil Lake are from 20 ft (6·1 m) at the entrance decreasing to 6 ft (1·8 m). It dries out at CD near the foot bridge (which can be opened by appointment by Admiralty police in gate house) and Forton Lake also dries out. The club house of the Gosport Cruising Club consists of old Gosport-Portsmouth ferry boats adjacent to the foot bridge and visitors can berth alongside.

(f) **Hardway**. See Chart page 94. This centre lies on the west side of the harbour about $\frac{1}{4}$ mile beyond the Sultan landing stage owned by the Admiralty, above the junction of Fareham and Portchester Lakes. Here the Hardway Sailing Club, Tel: Gosport 81875, is very active and hospitable. Every available space is now occupied by moorings off the club and to the north and south of it, on both sides of the channel. There is even an overflow of moorings for small cruising yachts in the entrance of Portchester and Bombketch Lakes. The mooring area near the club is protected from westerly winds and there is a public hard and pontoons. The sailing club maintains a visitors' trot of 5 fore and aft moorings off their pontoons, which has water laid on. There are so many other moorings that there is always the possibility of one being temporarily vacant, for which enquiry should be made at the club house. The club has a scrubbing grid, 6 ft (1·8 m) and launching site adjacent. Marine shop and fuels nearby. Other shops and pubs up the road facing the Hardway and a restaurant near Vosper's jetty. Short walk to bus stop for Gosport and Fareham.

(g) **Fareham and Portchester**—see next chapter.

Communications. Express trains from Portsmouth Harbour Station and Town Station. British Railway Ferries to Ryde, IoW, adjacent Harbour Station. Hovercraft from Harbour Station and Clarence Pier, Southsea. Car ferries to Wootton, IoW, from Camber. Buses from Portsmouth and Gosport ferry landings.

10.5. View from Hardway Club.

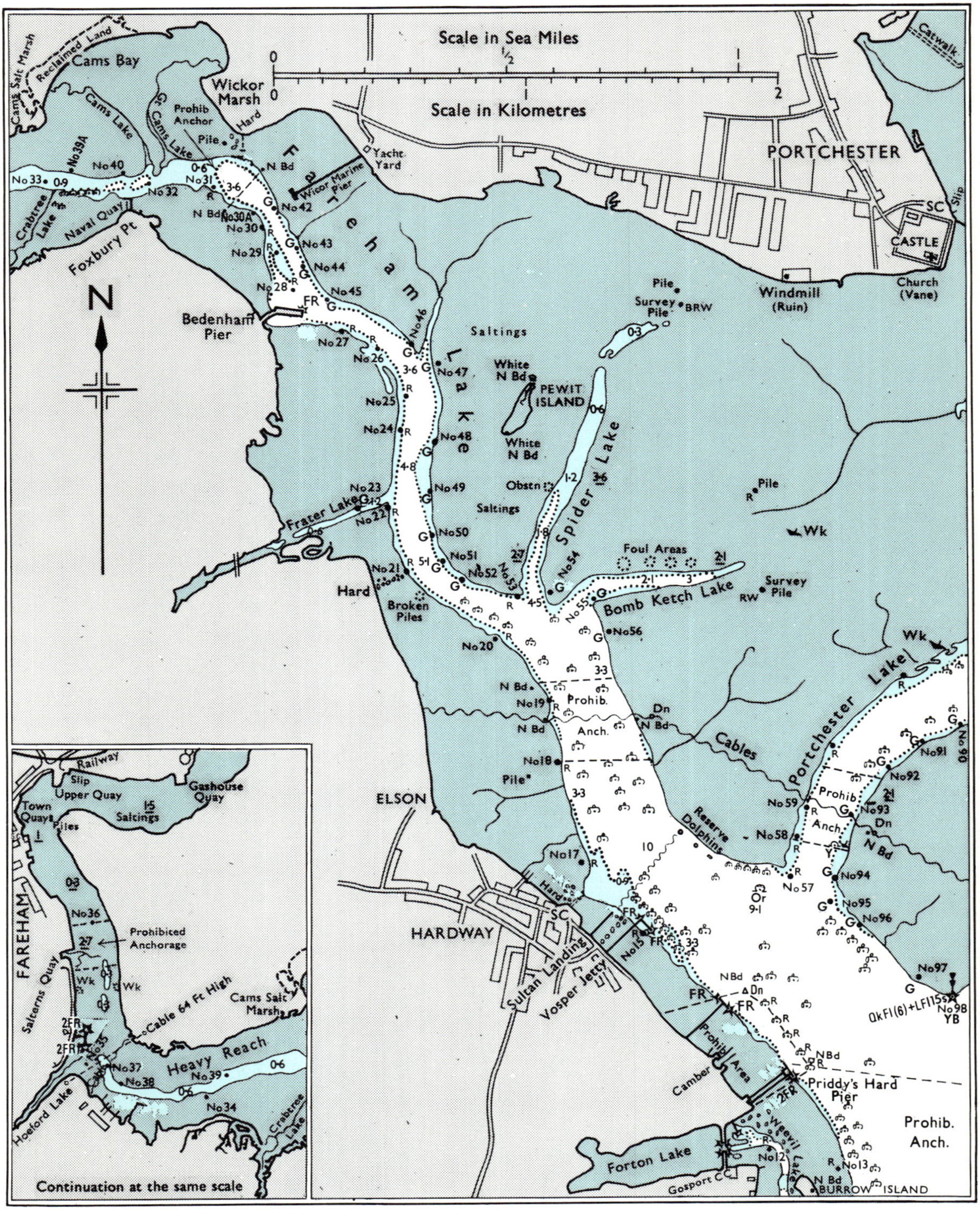

Fareham Lake: Soundings in metres. Add 0·5 m (1·8 ft) at MLWS, 1·5 m (5·0 ft) at MLWN. Based on British Admiralty Chart No. 2631, with the permission of HM Stationery Office and of the Hydrographer of the Navy.

11 Fareham and Portchester Lakes

High Water: About +0 h 20 m Portsmouth.
Tidal Heights: Fareham above datum: MHWS 13·2 ft (4·0 m) MLWS 1·8 ft (0·5 m) MHWN 10·5 ft (3·2 m) MLWN 5·0 ft (1·5 m).
Local streams: Shortly after HW the ebb runs for about $4\frac{3}{4}$ hours, followed by 3 hours slack before 4 hours flood.
Yacht Clubs: Fareham Sailing and Motor Boat Club, Portchester SC, Portsmouth Harbour Cruising Club.

Fareham Lake is the NW arm and Portchester Lake is the NE arm from the junction with the main channel in Portsmouth Harbour. Both channels (which are 'lakes' only at high water) provide considerable reaches for sailing, though they are used principally by yachts of small or moderate size.

Fareham is situated round an ancient settlement at the ford where the present River Wallington joins the creek. It suffered greatly from the ravages of the Vikings but survived and was mentioned in the Domesday Book, under the name of Fernham, when it was credited with one church and two mills. In recent years Fareham has grown a great deal and is a very busy small market town carrying the main road traffic between Portsmouth, Gosport and Southampton.

Historically, Portchester is of greater importance because of its castle, with walls dating from Roman times and enclosing a Norman church in an area of about nine acres. Throughout the Napoleonic wars many French and Spanish prisoners were confined there. The castle remains in an excellent state of preservation, dominated by the enormous keep, added by the Normans, from which a magnificent view of the yacht anchorage and the harbour is obtained.

FAREHAM LAKE

This is the continuation of the main channel above Hardway, which has already been referred to, and the Reserve Dolphins on the opposite side. It is a wide, deep water channel as far as Bedenham Pier and is clearly marked by red piles on the port hand and green piles to starboard. The piles should not be approached closely as some are on the mud banks which are very steep in most parts, but the edge is shoaling into the channel between No 48 and No 49 starboard hand pile. Avoid steering from one pile direct to the next as the mud sometimes edges into the channel between them, and do not take the bends too sharply. Bedenham Pier is Admiralty property and must not be approached within 40 ft (12·2 m). A quarter mile beyond this pier on the opposite (starboard) side is the yacht yard of Wicor Marine Ltd, with long pier and pontoon off which there are many

11.1. Reserver dolphins are to be left to starboard when sailing up Fareham Lake.

yacht moorings. Across from the pontoon is pile No 30A far up the mud which dries some 30 ft inside it, and where many yachts go aground. The lake then takes a turn round Wicor Bend to the west into Heavy Reach where the channel becomes narrower and leads between extensive mud banks. This reach is marked by occasional piles, but these are well up on the mud. Pilotage is easiest at half tide, but can be confusing at high water when the mud flats are covered. The bottom is uneven, ranging from 8 ft (2·4 m) down to as little as 4 ft (1·2 m) in parts. Naval yacht moorings run west from the Naval pier on the south side and there are moorings for small yachts in shallower water on the north side.

At Power Station bend at the end of this reach the Lake (now a creek) turns to north and passes under power cables with a clearance of 64 ft (19·5 m), MHWS. The channel, which dries out at CD, then leads almost straight up to Fareham, edging to starboard a little under the trees about halfway up the reach. The mooring buoys here should be kept close under the port side, as they are on this side of the channel practically as far up as the quays.

A number of subsidiary creeks join Fareham Lake. Most of these dry out or are of little interest to visiting yachtsmen, but mention may be made of **Bomb Ketch Lake** and **Spider Lake.** As will be seen on the chart, these lie on the east side and enter Fareham Lake at the same point, the entrances being separated only by a spit of mud on which stands the G pile (No 54). This should be left well to port and another G pile (No 55) to starboard if entering Bomb Ketch Lake. This creek leads east and has about 8 ft (2·4 m) least water for a distance of 3 cables, except for a small 6 ft (1·8 m) patch in the middle of the entrance. A few yachts are moored in the entrance, but anchorage at the eastern end is exposed at HW and the bottom is foul, besides being within the Tipner firing area. Spider Lake is entered between No 53 R pile to port and No 54 G pile to starboard. It leads about NNE for ½ mile with a least depth of 6 ft (1·8 m), decreasing to 3 ft (0·9 m) east of Peewit Island, and the upper reach is within the area of the Tipner rifle range. These lakes are far from facilities, are isolated and abound with birds and shellfish, as also does Peewit Island. Old Naval cannon from Tipner range have been recovered at LWS. There are many private moorings in the main channel between Spider Lake and Wicor Marine.

Frater Lake on the west side of Fareham Lake leads to Bedenham Naval Quays where landing is prohibited. In **Cams Lake** there are two creeks leading to opposite corners of the bay. They dry out at LW.

Moorings, Anchorage and Facilities

Anchorage out of the fairway is possible in Fareham Lake anywhere above Bedenham Pier, except in the prohibited areas west of the two notice boards and between Salterns Quay and No 36 pile, as shown on the chart, or in the vicinity of moorings. It is necessary to use a trip line as the bottom is foul in many parts and a riding light is necessary because of shingle barges. Except at Hardway, referred to under Portsmouth, the best chance of obtaining the temporarary use of a mooring is from the Wicor Marine Ltd, Tel: Fareham 237112, who have many moorings for shoal draft yachts and a few for yachts up to 6 ft (1·8 m) draft or more. Dry landing at pontoon at end of the long pier. Two slips and laying up and repairs undertaken. Chandlery, water and diesel, but far from shops.

Wicor Marine can launch from trailers craft of up to 7 tons displacement. Visiting yachts are welcome.

11.2. Fareham Creek up to the road bridge.

At Fareham small yachts have moorings. There is little water at LW springs but the bottom is soft mud and all except deep-keeled yachts will remain upright. Messrs R. & H. Hamper have a yacht building yard. Yachts of 6 ft (1·8 m) draft can proceed to the lower quay and yacht yard 2 hours either side of HW. Landing at pontoon at Fareham Sailing and Motor Boat Club, Tel: Fareham 280738. Water on application. Wilson's Fareham Marine, which is close by, caters for motor boats and has pontoons alongside lower quay. Launching site at public slipway alongside Wilson's Fareham Marine chandlers. In Fareham itself there are shops of all kinds, hotel and small restaurants and the facilities of a medium-sized town. EC Wednesday. Station and bus station. Market day Monday.

Fareham and Portchester Lakes

PORTCHESTER LAKE

Portchester Lake provides a good sailing area as the channel is wide and deep in its centre as far as Tipner Lake, but in parts there is only 9 to 10 ft (2·7 to 3·0 m), and much less near the edges. In the reach up to Portchester Castle, the bottom is even more irregular. Thus, although with local knowledge or with the aid of the large-scale No 2631 Admiralty Chart, 6 ft (1·8 m) CD may be found up to the Castle and 1½ cables beyond it, a stranger may find as little as 2 to 4 ft CD (0·6 to 1·2 m) in some parts of the defined channel. It is well marked by numbered piles, red to port, green to starboard. However, some of these are well up on the mud or in shallow water, so they should not be approached closely nor (as in Fareham Lake) should a course be steered direct from one to the next at LW.

When approaching from Portsmouth Harbour, before coming to the Reserve Dolphins, the red pile No 57 will be seen which marks the west side of the entrance to the Creek. The first reach, Long Reach, is not quite straight, although its general direction is NE. Off the entrance to Tipner Lake at the end of the reach on the east side, the main channel takes a turn to the NW. Here care should be taken as shallow water extends far beyond the No 67 pile on the port hand and there is a drying shoal on the starboard side between No 80 and No 79 piles. Here the best water is on the port hand off No 68 and No 69 piles, but beyond the latter the deepest water lies mid-channel, leading northwards past Portchester Castle. In this reach there are four large spherical yellow buoys marking water to be left clear for Hovercraft when operating from Vosper's shipyard, further up the lake.

Off Portchester Castle and above it, the deep centre of the channel is much narrower and ends north of Horsea Island where the whole area is being reclaimed. Several creeks join Portchester Lake but, except for dinghy sailing, the only major one is Tipner Lake.

Tipner Lake. This lake lies on the starboard side, where Portchester Lake turns westward about ½ mile south of Horsea Island. It is marked by channel posts, and the creek runs about easterly and passes through a prohibited anchorage before reaching Tipner Quays. Just before reaching these, there are drying moorings on the starboard side for shoal draft cruisers. Portsmouth Harbour Cruising Club has a landing at the drying concrete slip and water can be obtained at the club. On the port hand, opposite the quays, there is a small boat channel that links up with Langstone Harbour. After passing Tipner quays a smaller channel branches off on the starboard side and leads along under the shore to the end of the promenade. At half tide dinghies can land here, and it is only a short walk up the side-street to the buses which run to Portsmouth Guildhall.

Danger area. There is a danger area in Portchester Creek off Tipner Rifle Ranges which is shown on the chart and is defined by red notice boards. Red flags are flown at the Butts when firing is in progress, mostly at week-ends, and yachts are requested to

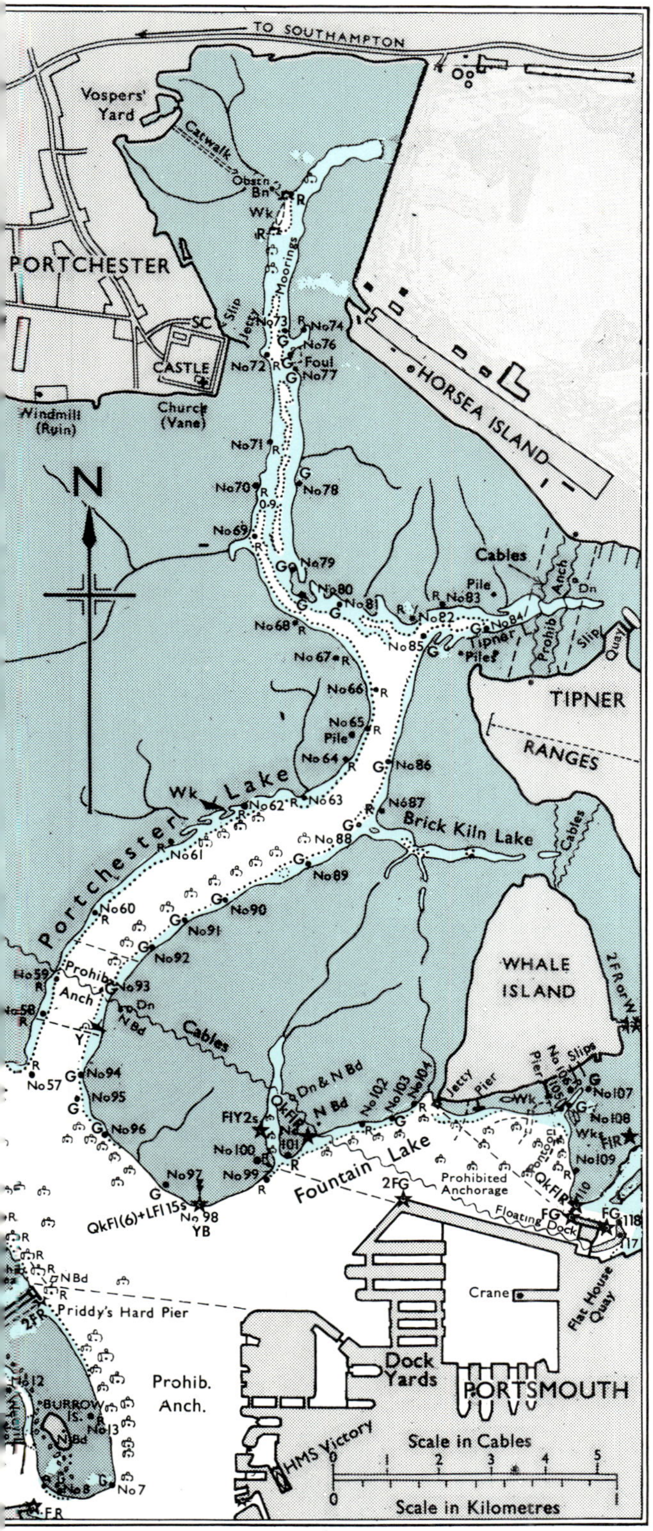

make passage through the area as quickly as possible.

Moorings, Anchorage and Facilities

The former anchorage, in rather poor holding ground in the channel south of the Castle, is now very limited as there are so many moorings that little room is left without encroaching upon the Hovercraft fairway. For the same reason, many of the yachts above the Castle are moored fore and aft so that they cannot swing into the fairway. Most of the moorings are licensed by the Portchester Sailing Club and let to their members. Application should be made to the duty officer of the club, which is helpful to visitors, to ascertain whether any moorings are temporarily vacant, but this cannot be counted on. It is reported that some silting is occurring above the Portchester reach, owing to less scour in the channel since the land reclamation farther up.

Landing at the north end of the Castle is made on the sailing club hard which has a concrete slip at the upper end. Yachts up to about $4\frac{1}{2}$ ft (1·4 m) draft with their own legs can be scrubbed here with a 14 ft (3·6 m) tide, and it also provides a launching site. The sailing club is in the Old Vicarage, alongside the hard, Tel: Cosham 76375. Water at tap near the Priory Church or on application at the club. There is a public

Portchester Lake: Soundings in metres. Add 0·5 m (1·8 ft) at MLWS, 1·5 m (5·0 ft) at MLWN. Based on British Admiralty Chart No. 2631, with the permission of HM Stationery Office and of the Hydrographer of the Navy.

car park and toilets about 100 yards from hard and the sailing club has its own car park. In the old village near the Castle is the Cormorant Inn and small shops, and $\frac{3}{4}$ mile up the road there are more shops, a PO, café, garage and bus stop. EC on Tuesday or for some shops Wednesday. The Castle is very well worth a visit.

11.3. View from Portchester Castle Keep over the Priory Church to Portchester Lake and Portsmouth beyond.

12 Bembridge Harbour

High Water (Long): −0 h 5 m Portsmouth.
Tidal Heights above datum: Outside the harbour approximately as at Portsmouth. Within harbour: MHWS 10·1 ft (3·3 m) MLWS 0·1 ft (0·3 m) MHWN 7·6 ft (2·3 m) MLWN 1·3 ft (0·4 m).
Stream sets ½ mile E of St Helens Fort weakly to S at +2 h 0 m Portsmouth, SE +4 h 0 m, S +6 h 0 m, NW −3 h 15 m, W −2 h 0 m, WSW +1 h 30 m.
Depths: Most of the channel between the sands dries out at CD, except near the inner entrance. Within the harbour itself, which is shallow, water is impounded at very low spring tides. There is a dredged area at St Helens.
Yacht Clubs: Bembridge SC, Brading Haven YC.

Bembridge Harbour or Brading Haven, as it used to be known, is the most easterly of the Island harbours. It is a natural formation sheltered from the prevailing winds and with good facilities. The wide clean sands in the approach, fishing and shrimping and walks to the Foreland make Bembridge a good centre for the family yachtsman. In the days of sail St Helens Road provided an anchorage for the assembly of British fleets, and water casks were filled from a spring at Bembridge. The Road was the scene of the Spithead mutiny in 1797.

The disadvantage is that the entrance channel and the harbour itself are so shallow that they are suitable only for shallow draft yachts except near HW. However, the Bembridge Harbour Improvement Company Limited, who bought all harbour rights from British Railways, are gradually improving the yachting amenities.

The Approach and Entrance

The approach to Bembridge is from a NE direction to the yellow beacon *Qk Fl Y* situated about 2 cables west of St Helens Fort *Gp Fl (3) 10 sec*, which is left about 1½ cable to SE. There is a tide gauge on the beacon which indicates the depth of water over the shallowest section of the channel, which is in the vicinity of Nos 8 and 9 buoys. The channel has changed and the tide guage, which used to be a starboard hand beacon with triangular top-mark, is now outside the channel and should be left to port. It is now painted yellow and is to have a yellow saltire top-mark fitted. The entrance to the channel is near the tide gauge and is marked by two buoys, No 1 conical green to starboard and No 2 can red to port. From here on the course to be taken is marked by green conical buoys with odd numbers to starboard and by red can buoys with even numbers to port. Their position is altered to suit the changing course of the channel and is only approximately shown on the chartlet. The channel becomes narrower and deeper as No 11 starboard hand buoy is approached. Ahead lies a pool where many club boats lie at moorings. To the east may be seen the conspicuous buildings of the erstwhile Royal Spithead Hotel and the Bembridge Sailing Club.

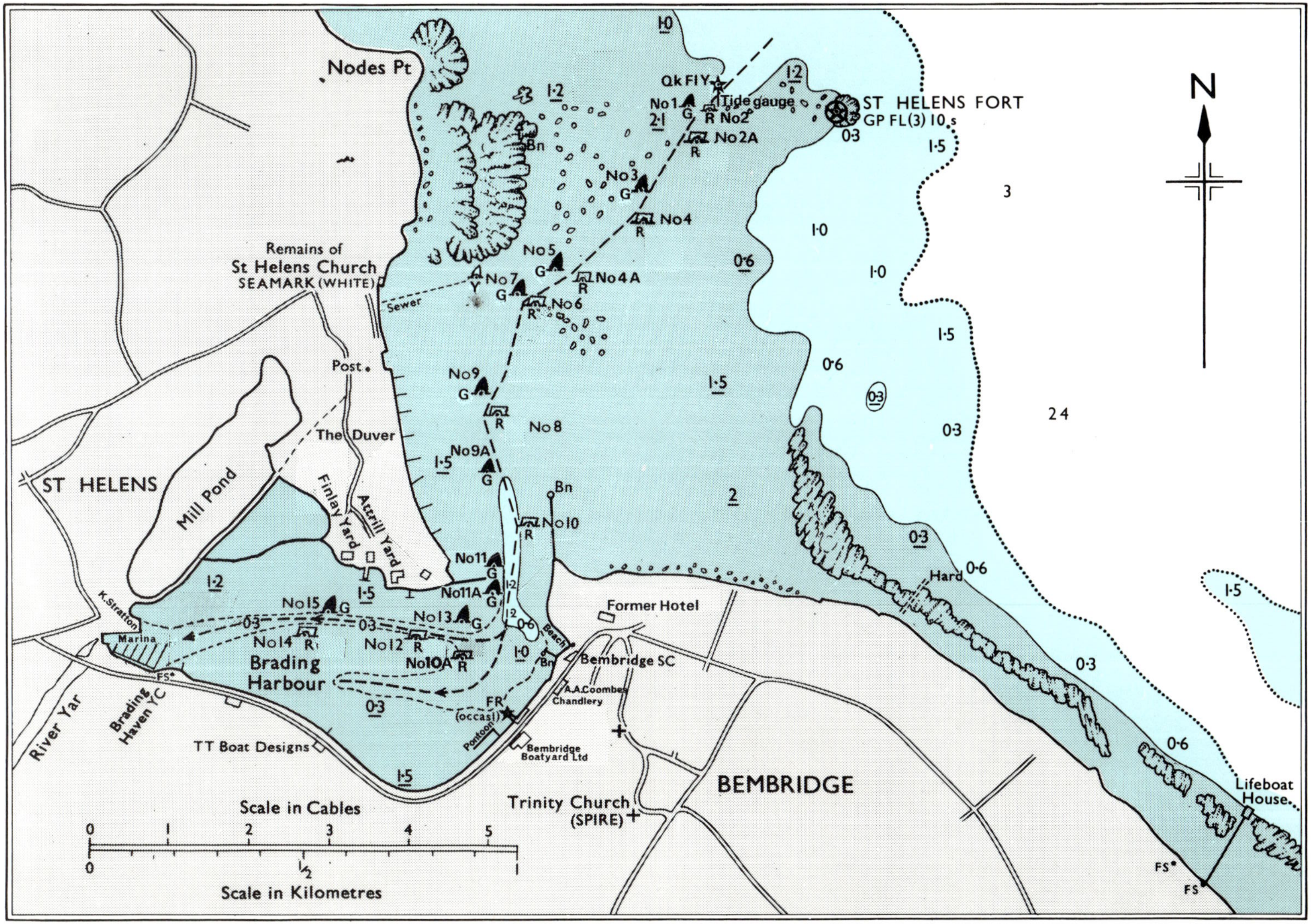

Bembridge Harbour: Soundings in metres. Add 0·03 m (0·1 ft) at MLWS, 0·4 m (1·3 ft) at MLWN. Based on Bembridge Harbour Improvement Co Ltd plan and on British Admiralty Chart No. 2050, with the permission of HM Stationery Office and of the Hydrographer of the Navy and of the Bembridge Harbour Improvement Co.

12.1. St. Helens Fort which should be left about one and a half cables to port when approaching.

The main channel to Bembridge Marina at St Helen's Quay leads in a westerly direction and is marked on the starboard side by Nos 13 and 15 green conical buoys and on the port side by Nos 10A, 12 and 14 red can buoys.

12.2. The approach to Bembridge Haven with the tide guage and the two buoys that mark the entrance to the channel. St Helen's Seamark can be seen between them.

Bembridge Harbour

The harbour is administed by the Bembridge Harbour Improvements Co Ltd. General Manager (in which the position of Harbour Master is vested)—Major S. C. Selwyn MBE (Tel: Bembridge 2828).

Lights: The only permanent light is the *Qk Fl* Yellow light on the beacon at the entrance.

12.3. Facing east showing the steep bank on the port hand and the notice board directing visitors to St Helen's Quay.

Anchorage, Moorings and Facilities

The best anchorage outside the harbour is at Under Tyne off the Bembridge SC starting line, less than ½ mile east of the former Royal Spithead Hotel. This position is well protected from winds from south to west, though exposed if the wind veers to NW and other directions. Anchor outside the permanent moorings in sufficient depth of water and buoy the anchor. The hard shown on the chart is more in the nature of a landing place between the rocks but at HW land on the beach whence follow the shore to Bembridge.

A number of visitors' berths are available at the marina, where only one or two feet of water can be expected at LW, but below is soft mud and craft up to 6 feet draught usually remain upright. Accommodation at the marina is very limited on Saturday nights and during the holiday period, so it is advisable to get in as early as possible on the tide leaving a margin for departure if necessary. Berthing Master—Mr R. (Bob) Green (Tel: Bembridge 2973 at HW, 3635 at LW).

Craft that can take the ground are permitted to anchor fore-and-aft on the beach immediately to port on entering the inner harbour if there is space available. Anchoring elsewhere in the harbour is prohibited.

There is some visitors' accommodation at the Bembridge Boatyard Ltd pontoon (Tel: Bembridge 2423) and drying moorings may be available from A. A. Coombes (Tel: Bembridge 2296) or from Attrill's Yard (Tel: Bembridge 2319).

12.4. The pontoon of Attrill's Yard on the north side of the harbour.

Bembridge Harbour

The Brading Haven YC adjoins the Quay and temporary members are welcomed. There are small shops at St Helens, $\frac{1}{4}$ mile distant up the hill. EC varies but PO Saturdays. Bembridge itself is nearly $\frac{3}{4}$ mile along the south harbour. Here there are hotels, restaurants and shops. EC Thursday.

Bembridge is an active racing centre with several yacht yards: Attrill's and Finlay's on the St Helens side of the harbour and Coombes, TT Boat Designs and Bembridge Boatyard Ltd on the south side. Chandlery at Coombes and yacht yards. Diesel fuel may be obtained from Bembridge Boatyard Ltd, from K. Stratton beside the marina and, subject to their own needs, from the jetties and pontoons off Attrill's and Finlay's yards. Petrol can be had from Bembridge Motor Services Ltd, next to Bembridge Boatyard Ltd. Launching sites: concrete ramp near St Helen's Church seamark (for about 3 hours either side of HW), and from sands and beaches, or by arrangement with yacht yards or at clubs by permission only. Buses to Ryde and all parts of the Island.

12.5. St. Helens Marina in the centre and the quay to the right.

13 Langstone Harbour

High Water: +0 h 5 m Portsmouth.
Tidal Heights above datum: Approx MHWS 15·8 ft (4·8 m) MLWS 2·1 ft (0·6 m) MHWN 12·7 ft (3·9 m) MLWN 5·9 ft (1·8 m).
Stream sets in Hayling Bay rotary anti-clockwise 075° at about +5 h 45 m Portsmouth; 360° at −4 h 0 m; 315° at −2 h 0 m; 280° at HW; 260° at +1 h 0 m; 230° at +2 h 0 m; 160° at +2 h 30 m; 130° at +4 h 0 m; 110° at +5 h 30 m. Streams weak with maximum 0·9 knot HW to +1 h 0 m and 0·7 knot −5 h 0 m.
Depths: The depth of water on the inner Langstone Bar varies from time to time and has been about 6 ft (1·8 m) at CD, with as little as 2 ft (0·6 m) outside on the southern hook of the East Winner. Within the harbour there are reaches with 6 ft (1·8 m) and more—see chart.
Yacht Clubs: Locks SC, Tudor SC, Eastney Cruising Association.

Langstone has always been a somewhat neglected harbour and during the French wars it was much used as a retreat for privateers seeking to avoid pursuit in the English Channel. The inhabitants of Hayling Island were once well known for smuggling and wrecking.

The days of privateers, smugglers and other colourful characters have passed but the lonely backwaters which they frequented still remain. There are creeks where the only sound comes from the seabirds, and reaches in the Langstone Channel where it is still possible to find room for cruising yachts to anchor in 6 ft (1·8 m) and over, though far from shore facilities. The harbour provides a good cruising area for dinghy sailing and there is plenty of active small boat racing.

The bar and the Winner sands, on which innumerable vessels have been driven ashore, have given the approach a bad reputation, but in normal summer weather and on the flood tide the entrance presents no particular problems. It is in fact easier than Chichester Harbour entrance.

The Approach and Entrance

The approach from the Solent presents no difficulties. Hold a course past the Horse Sand Fort to clear the nearby shoal shown on the chart and the submerged barrier. Then steer NE to bring the Horse Sand Fort into line astern with Noman's Land Fort, whence keep on this transit steering 055°. This leads (in the direction of the prominent Royal Hotel almost midway on the front of Hayling Island) to Langstone red Fairway buoy *Gp Fl (2) R 10s*, distance about 2¼ miles. A beacon marking a dangerous wreck will be left to port and an obstruction (4 ft at CD) is left to starboard. If there is fog take care not to overstand the Langstone buoy.

If proceeding from Portsmouth the short cut may be taken through the gap in the barrier marked by a pile on an obstruction on the north side and a dolphin *Qk Fl R* on the south. This carries 4 ft (1·2 m) CD. Then steer 079° for Langstone buoy heading midway between the conspicuous hotel and Eastoke Pt. The course leaves the wreck to starboard

13.1. The dolphin marking the south side of the passage through the submerged barrier between Southsea and Horse Sand Fort.

and leads just north of Langstone buoy. Alter course when it is sighted to leave it to port. There is also a second passage known as the 'Boat Passage' through the submerged barrier. This lies close inshore and is marked by beacons. The depth is only 3 ft (0·9 m) CD, and 2 ft (0·6 m) east of it.

13.2. Langstone Fairway buoy. The entrance is just to the left of the buoy in the background.

13.3. The conspicuous chimney on the west side of Langstone entrance and the two dolphins with beacons which give a useful transit.

Approaching from the eastward the hook-shaped extension of the East Winner extends over 1½ miles from the shore, with depths as little as 2 ft (0·6 m) CD, at its extremity off which lies the East Winner South cardinal buoy (yellow/black unlit). These shoals (which frequently shift after gales and tend to lengthen) may be cleared in about 6 ft (1·8 m) CD, by keeping Haslar hospital open southward of Southsea Castle, until the Fairway buoy comes into line with the east side of Langstone harbour entrance. Then steer for the buoy leaving it to port. Here the in-going stream begins +5 h 40 m Portsmouth to the NE, gradually turning anti-clockwise to end WNW at high water. The maximum spring rate of 1·2 knots, direction 325° from −2 h 0 m for an hour. The out-going begins to the south at +1 h 20 m and attains maximum spring rate 2·1 knots S by E at +3 h 0 m, ending easterly. The streams tend to follow the channel when the sands are uncovered and are stronger as the entrance, which is very deep, is approached. Here a spring rate of 3·5 knots is attained in the entrance on the flood (but there is an hour's slack at about half tide) and 4½ knots (sometimes more) on the ebb which begins at +0 h 25 m Portsmouth.

From the Fairway Buoy a course should be steered to the middle of the entrance between the sands, allowing for any athwartship tide. Alternatively, bring the beacons on the two dolphins on the west side of the entrance into line at about 344° and follow this transit, bearing to starboard ¼ mile before reaching the entrance, when the channel is obvious.

The easiest time of approach in good weather is on the young flood before the East Winner (which is fairly steep-to) is covered so that the direction of the channel can be seen. At this state of the tide the East or West Winner afford some protection to the channel except during onshore winds. Nearer high tide there is of course more water and

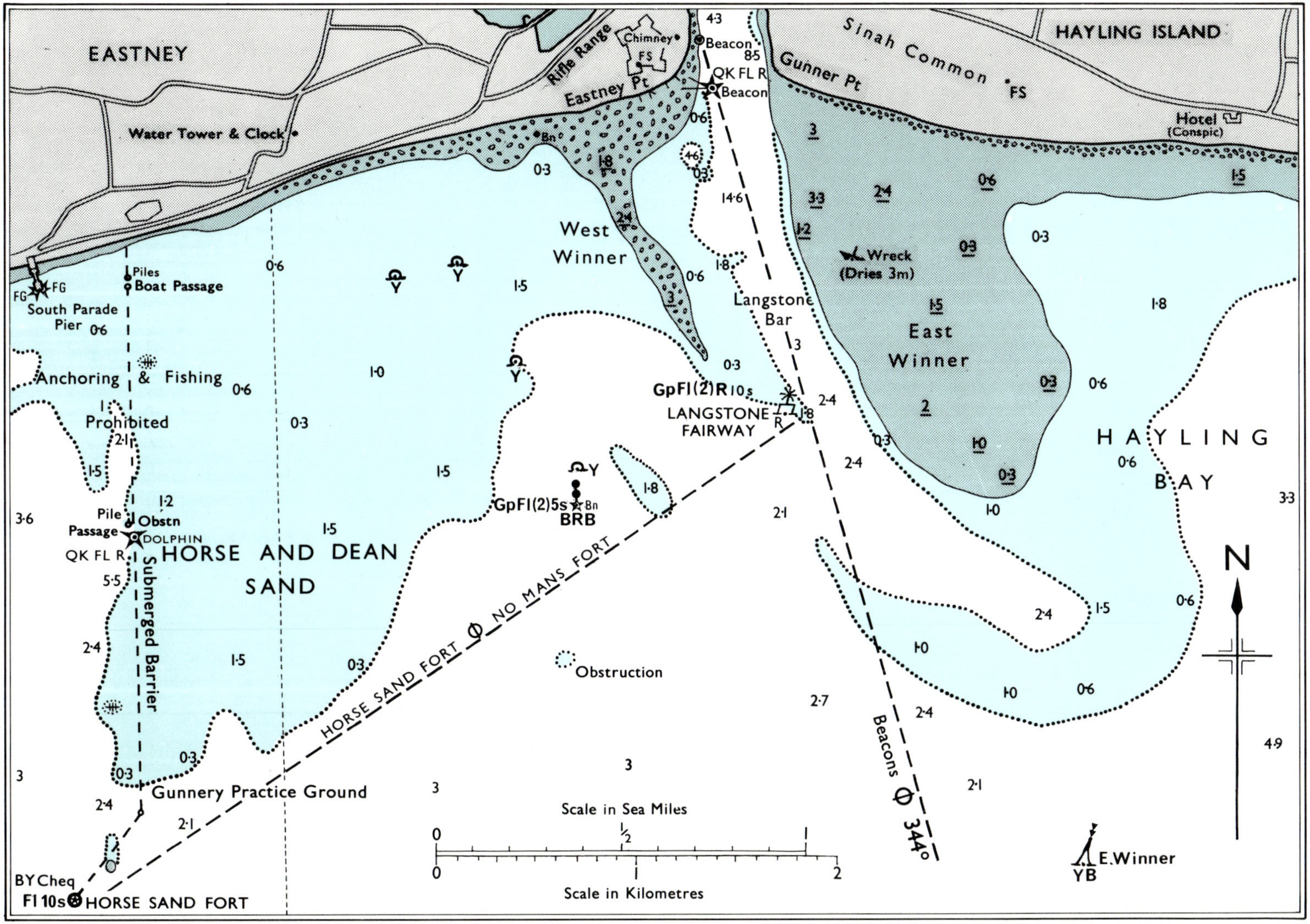

Entrance of Langstone Harbour: Soundings in metres. Add 0·6 m (2·1 ft) at MLWS, 1·8 m (5·9 ft) at MLWN. Based on British Admiralty Chart No. 3418, with the permission of HM Stationery Office and of the Hydrographer of the Navy.

the East Winner can often be identified by the seas breaking on the sands: in bad weather they are covered by a mass of breaking water. During strong onshore winds and gales Langstone Harbour should not be approached as the seas break on the bar and in the shoal water far south of the Fairway buoy. The East Winner is a lee shore in south and SW winds; on the ebb tide under gale conditions it is particularly dangerous. Even in good weather entry on the ebb should be avoided if possible owing to the strength of the stream in and near the entrance.

At the top of the narrows at the entrance, pontoons for the ferries will be seen on either hand, and once past these the harbour widens out into a tidal lake over 2 miles across, congested with sand and mud banks, but intersected with channels and small creeks.

Gunnery Practice: There is a rifle range at Eastney, with danger area SW towards the gap in the Barrier. The Fraser Gunnery Range, covering approaches to Langstone and Chichester harbours, is at Eastney Point SW of the chimney. **Danger Signals** displayed 30 m before and while firing. Large red flag above International Pendant 1 for **area 1** (200 yards 120° to 200°). Above Pendant 2 for **area 2** (6000 yards 120° to 155°). Above Pendant 3 for **area 3** (12,500 yards 120° to 155°). Above Pendant 4 for **area 4** (24,000 yards 126° to 146°). Areas 2, 3 and 4 with lethal ammunition. Signals displayed from range building, SW corner South Parade Pier, W side Langstone entrance, Harbour Master's Office and Selsey CG. Naval Patrol boat, flying red flag is stationed close to danger areas when areas 2, 3, and 4 in use. Normal hours 1300-1530 Monday to Friday, but forenoon used when weather on previous days unsuitable.

Lights: After rounding the Fairway buoy *Gp Fl (2) R 10s*, the entrance can usually be seen at night against the lights on Portsdown Hill and there is a *Qk Fl R* light on the outer beacon at the entrance and another *Fl R* 4 cables north also on the west side. Within the harbour there is a light on the port hand E Milton buoy *Gp Fl (4) R 10s* and opposite on the starboard hand NW Sinah buoy *Fl 5s*. These lights assist in the approach channel. There is also a light *Fl R* in the Broom Channel at the entrance of Salterns Lake and there are three lit beacons in the Langstone Channel, bearing the letters 'A', 'B' and 'C'.

THE MAIN CHANNEL AND HARBOUR

Within the entrance the main channel, which runs in a northerly direction, is wide and deep. On the west side it is joined at the entrance by Eastney Lake and on the east by Sinah Lake. Northward of these creeks the channel is very wide and there are many orange mooring buoys in deep water on the port side and an increasing number on the starboard hand in the vicinity of the concrete Mulberry grounded on the west of Sinah Sands. About 1½ cables beyond this is the previously mentioned green conical starboard hand NW Sinah buoy, and on the opposite side the red port hand E Milton buoy. The deepest water is on the west side of the channel. There is plenty of water in the fairway marked for the dredgers between the two light buoys, though there is a small 1 ft (0·3 m) shoal about 2 cables south of the NW Sinah buoy.

Beyond these buoys the Langstone Channel, which is deep for nearly two miles, branches off to the NE but the main channel continues northward for another ½ mile before branching into the Broom Channel which continues NW to the road embankment north of Portsea Island.

Perches within the harbour have a high casualty rate due to oyster dredging and many are either missing altogether or are without their top-mark.

Owing to the number of moorings and the narrow fairway left for the gravel dredgers and ships proceeding to Kendall's Wharf, there is no room left for anchoring in the main channel. Anchorage is now only practicable in the Langstone Channel and Russell's Lake but see below—shallow draft yachts such as twin-keelers or multi-hullers can explore and find anchorages out of the fairways and in minor creeks not available to yachts of deeper draft.

13.4. Visitors' moorings, Harbour Master's office, Ferryboat Inn and ferry pontoon on the east side of the entrance.

Moorings, Anchorage and Facilities

There are six visitors' moorings for temporary use on the east side of the entrance, south of the notice board indicating where the cables cross. The position is exposed and very uncomfortable in high winds. In case of SE winds of much strength there is said to be a danger of these moorings dragging off the shelf and into the deep water of the channel; the ebb could then take one out to the Winner, mooring and all! It is best to go ashore to consult the Harbour Master who will advise whether any of the numerous moorings in the harbour are available for a longer stay and give any other information required. The Harbour Master, Mr H. J. Owen has an office in a Rollalong cabin nearby on the Hayling side of the ferry (Tel: Hayling Island 3419) and will advise visiting yachtsmen on moorings, use of launching site or other facilities.

His office is open from 9 a.m. until 5 p.m.

Water Ski-ing: Water ski-ing is permitted within certain areas specified from time to time in Local Notices to Mariners. There is a water ski-ing area marked with yellow buoys and perches over the shoal sands either side of the Langstone Channel. Landing places within the entrance to west and east for the towing power craft are also specified. There is a speed limit of 10 knots in the entrance.

Sinah Lake

Sinah Lake is on the Hayling Island side just within the entrance. All the best positions are occupied by moorings as is the Kench, the small bay on the south side, which dries out at low water.

It is best to enter Sinah Lake close to the ferry pontoon where there is 1 ft (0·3 m) CD whereas farther northward the sands dry out over a cable south of the Mulberry. Care

13.5. The stranded concrete 'mulberry' on the east side of the harbour. There is shallow water to the south of it and a shoal about a cable west and beyond.

should be taken to avoid being set against the ferry pontoon where the stream is strong, especially on the ebb 2 hours after HW when it attains nearly 5 knots at springs. The channel runs at first in a NE by E direction and deepens to over a fathom north of the Kench. There is an inner bar which dries out as shown on the chart, and then a ½ mile reach to E and NE with depths ranging from 8 ft (2·4 m) down to 3 ft (0·9 m) CD at the eastern end. There are few marks to aid pilotage in the western part of Sinah Lake other than the yachts on moorings which show the trend of the channel, but some of these are shallow draft so keep close to the line of the larger yachts. The upper reaches are perched and lead to the Rod Rythe creek (which joins Sinah Lake to the Langstone Channel) and is also marked by perches. This provides a short cut which can be used by dinghies and shallow craft and is stated locally to be navigable by yachts at about half tide.

There is no room available in Sinah Lake for anchoring, so the visiting yachtsman should apply to the Harbour Master at Ferry Point for the use of a vacant mooring if any is available.

At Sinah there is the Ferry Boat Inn, and a café which supplies stores in summer. Water point behind Inn, or from Boat-harbour Company opposite Inn who also supply fuel. Harbour Master's office and workshop adjacent. Launching site on slip. Car park nearby. Bus service to Hayling Village in summer, where there are hotels, shops and PO. EC Wednesday. Frequent ferries in daylight hours to Eastney, thence summer bus service to Southsea.

Eastney Lake or the Locks

This shallow lake lies just inside the entrance of Langstone Harbour on the west side, opposite Sinah Lake. To enter the lake an incoming vessel should pass between the Ferry Pontoon and the first Royal Marine mooring buoy. Then the buoy should be kept straight on her stern, and course steered almost west (Mag), in the passage between the craft moored on each side of the creek. This creek should be approached with *caution* as the channel is narrow and is congested with moorings for small craft. There are local boatmen from whom advice or assistance may be obtained.

There is another channel running south just inside the Ferry point, at the entrance of Eastney Lake, but this is very shallow. The middle of the lake is blocked by a large mud flat.

The Locks Sailing Club house is situated at Milton Locks on the north side of Eastney Lake; it is an active club and holds numerous dinghy races during the summer. There is a hard just north of the locks, and a general stores up the road. EC Wednesday. Easy connections with Southsea and Portsmouth. Launching site at end of road near Ferry pontoon.

Milton or Velder Lake is the next shallow creek north of Eastney Lake on the west side of the main channel, but is of little significance as it leads only to an area of reclaimed land.

Broom Channel

This continuation of the main channel in a NW direction to Hillsea is used by ballast dredgers as far as Kendall's Wharf. It is comparatively narrow but carries 7 ft (2·1 m) of water for the first ½ mile, though it shoals quickly about 2 cables south of Kendall's

Langstone Harbour: Soundings in metres. Add 0·6 m (2·1 ft) at MLWS, 1·8 m (5·9 ft) at MLWN. Based on British Admiralty Chart No. 3418, with the permission of HM Stationery Office and of the Hydrographer of the Navy.

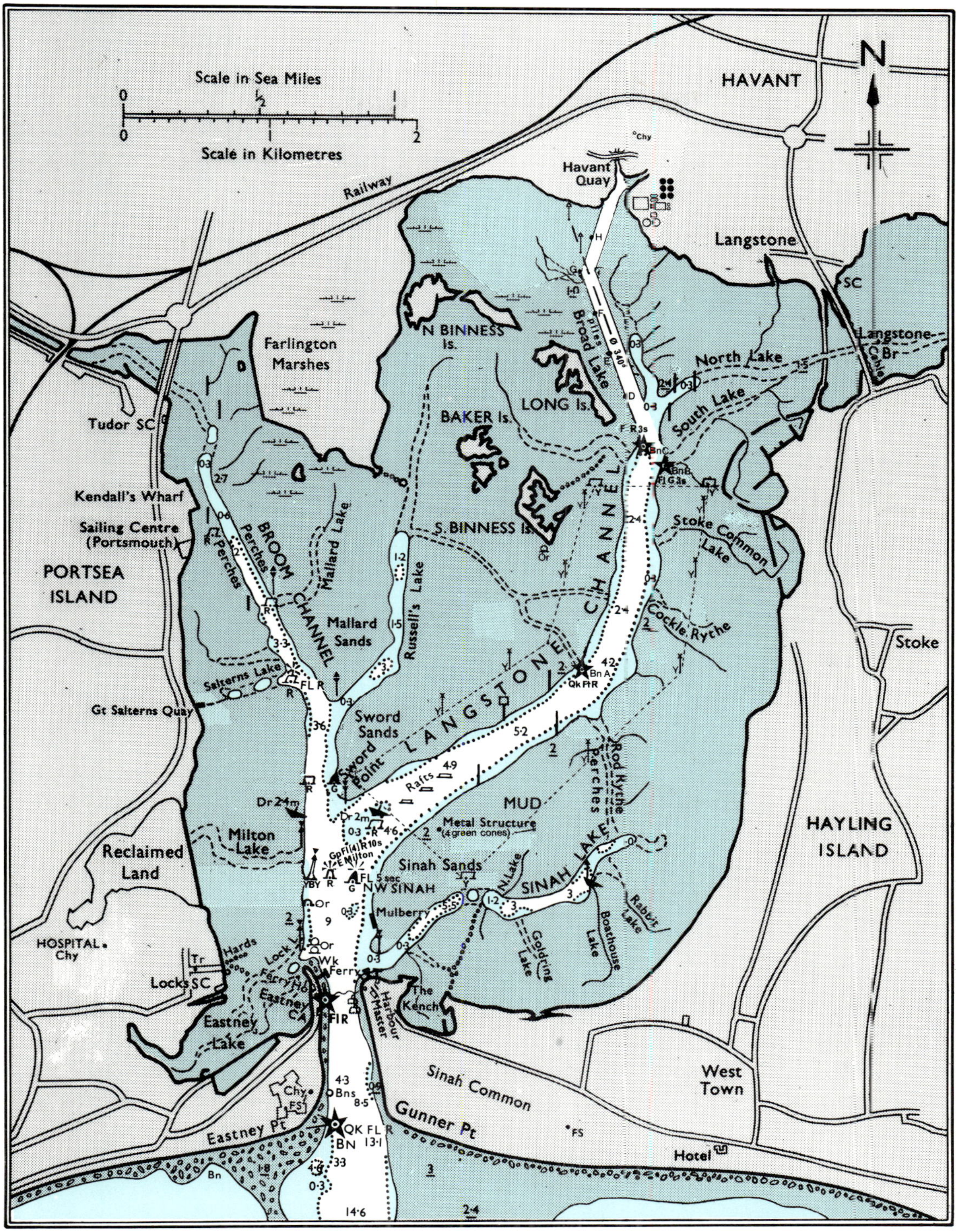
Scale in Sea Miles
Scale in Kilometres
HAVANT
N
Havant Quay
Langstone
SC
Langstone Br
Railway
Farlington Marshes
N BINNESS Is.
Broad Lake
North Lake
South Lake
LONG Is.
BAKER Is.
Tudor SC
Kendall's Wharf
Sailing Centre (Portsmouth)
PORTSEA ISLAND
BROOM CHANNEL
Perches
Mallard Lake
S. BINNESS Is.
Stoke Common Lake
Russell's Lake
Mallard Sands
CHANNEL
Cockle Ryche
Stoke
LANGSTONE
Salterns Lake
Gt Salterns Quay
Sword Sands
Sword Point
Rafts
MUD
Rod Ryche Perches
Metal Structure (4 green cones)
HAYLING ISLAND
Milton Lake
Reclaimed Land
Sinah Sands
NW SINAH
SINAH LAKE
Mulberry
Golding Lake
Boathouse Lake
Rabbit Lake
HOSPITAL Chy
Locks SC
Hards
Lock L
Ferry
Eastney Lake
The Kench
Harbour Master
Sinah Common
West Town
Eastney Pt
Gunner Pt
Hotel

Wharf and dries out at chart datum a cable beyond. It is marked by perches on the mud on either side and 3 buoys. The Tudor Sailing Club is situated at the northern end of this channel near the road bridge and has many moorings for shallow draft craft. Half a mile to the south is the Portsmouth Sailing Centre.

There is no room for anchoring in the deeper part of Broom Channel below Kendall's Wharf as the fairway is used by the ballast dredgers. Apply to the Tudor SC to ascertain whether a visitor's mooring is available, preferably at neaps when there is more water.

Russell's Lake joins Broom Channel on the east side and runs between mud flats to Farlington Marshes. It is only 1 ft (0·3 m) CD in the entrance but is wide and has deeper pools with from 5 ft (1·5 m) to 10 ft (3·0 m). It is marked by occasional perches. The pools provide quiet, though rather remote, anchorages.

Saltern's Lake lies on the west side of the Broom Channel. It has a red buoy *Fl R* at the entrance and perches mark the channel. It is no longer used by ballast dredgers and is largely filled by yacht moorings.

LANGSTONE CHANNEL

The entrance of this channel lies northward of the Sinah sands and the NW Sinah green conical light buoy. There is a middle ground in the entrance with as little as 1 ft (0·3 m) CD and a wreck marked by a red buoy 'IRISHMAN WRECK'. The easiest entry is south of this shoal, approaching from the NW Sinah buoy and treating the wreck buoy and four moored Admiralty rafts as port hand marks. Leave to starboard the metal structures which are well up on Sinah sands.

The channel is wide and deep, ranging from 18 to 9 ft (5·5 to 2·7 m) for the first mile. It runs in a NE direction and is marked by occasional perches. The yellow buoys are water ski-ing marks, sometimes in shallow water, and are of no navigational significance though they may help to indicate the general direction of the channel. About a mile from the entrance there is the first of seven pile beacons indicating the channel to Havant Quay and marked 'A' to 'H', 'A', 'B' and 'C' being lit.

North Lake and South Lake both dry out and lead easterly through the gap in the former railway bridge to Hayling road bridge. North Lake is the better marked of the two and navigable with sufficient rise of tide if proceeding to Chichester Harbour. The road bridge can only be passed under by craft without masts as there is no more than 7 ft (2·1 m) clearance below it at high water springs and the stream is strong. The span of the bridge with the best water under it is marked on the pile on the north side with a black diamond on a white background with black bands below it and by a black triangle on the south side. For Langstone village see Chichester Harbour.

13.7. Hayling Island road bridge separates Langstone and Chichester harbours.

There is plenty of room to anchor in Langstone Channel, which is quiet except in strong winds against the tide or when water ski-ing is in progress. The best holding ground is on the north side beyond the rafts, little more than a mile from the Locks SC which is not far by dinghy with outboard engine in ordinary weather. However it is important to anchor well clear of the channel, as the dredgers that ply to Havant Quay have, it is said, scant respect for anchored yachts.

14 Chichester Harbour

High Water: At entrance +0 h 5 m Portsmouth.
Tidal Heights above datum: Entrance MHWS 16·2 ft (4·9 m) MLWS 2·3 ft (0·7 m) MHWN 13 ft (3·9 m) MLWN 6 ft (1·8 m).
Stream sets to westward 2·1 miles S of Cakeham Tower at 1 knot maximum −2 h 0 m Portsmouth. Begins about NW rotating anti-clockwise to finish S, and easterly stream begins +5 h 0 m Portsmouth. For Hayling Bay see Langstone Harbour.
Depths: Bar has 1 ft (0·3 m) which is over 3 ft at MLWS, but depths and sands vary from time to time. Channel at entrance very deep. Inner bar NE of the NW Winner Buoy 5 ft (1·5 m) to 7 ft (2·1 m). In Chichester Channel depths vary from 9 ft (2·7 m) upwards as far as Itchenor.
Yacht Clubs: Birdham YC, Bosham SC, Chichester YC, Emsworth SC, Emsworth Cruising Association, Emsworth Slipper SC, Dell Quay SC, Hayling Island SC, Itchenor SC, Langstone SC, Mengham Rythe SC, Thorney Island SC (RAF), West Wittering SC.

Chichester is one of the largest and most concentrated yachting centres in the South of England. This is not surprising as it provides a cruising area in itself, with several miles of sheltered water in its four main channels: Emsworth, Thorney, Bosham and Chichester. Besides this, all the creeks and harbours of the Solent are within easy reach and it is a good point for departure to France or more extended cruises. It is also a great centre for dinghy and other racing. Within the harbour there is a speed limit of 6 knots for yachts under power.

Historically, the harbour has associations deeply rooted in the past for it was known to Roman, Saxon and Dane. At one time there was a monastery in the village of Bosham and the largest bell was seized and carried away by the Danes on one of their numerous raids. Legend has it that no sooner had the raiders departed than the monks returned to the belfry and began a peal. The missing note came ringing over the water from the Danish vessel, over a mile away in Bosham Deep; then the bottom of the raider's ship opened, the bell sank, and the planks of their vessel closed together again. According to the legend the bell could only be recovered by a team of pure white heifers. Today, a replica of the bell is seen on the burgees of members of the Bosham Sailing Club in all parts of the harbour, but, to date, the team of white heifers has remained lacking.

The Approach, Bar and Entrance

There are extensive shoals off the entrance to Chichester, and large parts dry out at low water. On the west side there are the West Pole sands and on the east side the Middle Pole and East Pole sands which extend nearly 1½ miles off the shore. Three-quarters of a mile off the entrance is the bar which varies from time to time in position and depth.

At the time of writing the bar carries 1 ft (0·3 m) at CD (over 3 ft MLWS), and is in effect a continuation of the Middle Pole which dries −1 ft (−0·3 m). An incoming yacht must wait for sufficient rise of tide to cross the bar with an adequate factor of safety, especially in rough weather or a swell. In normal weather with reasonable visibility there is no difficulty about approach and entry after half flood, but the ebb attains a spring rate of well over 5 knots at the entrance. A yacht under sail cannot make headway against

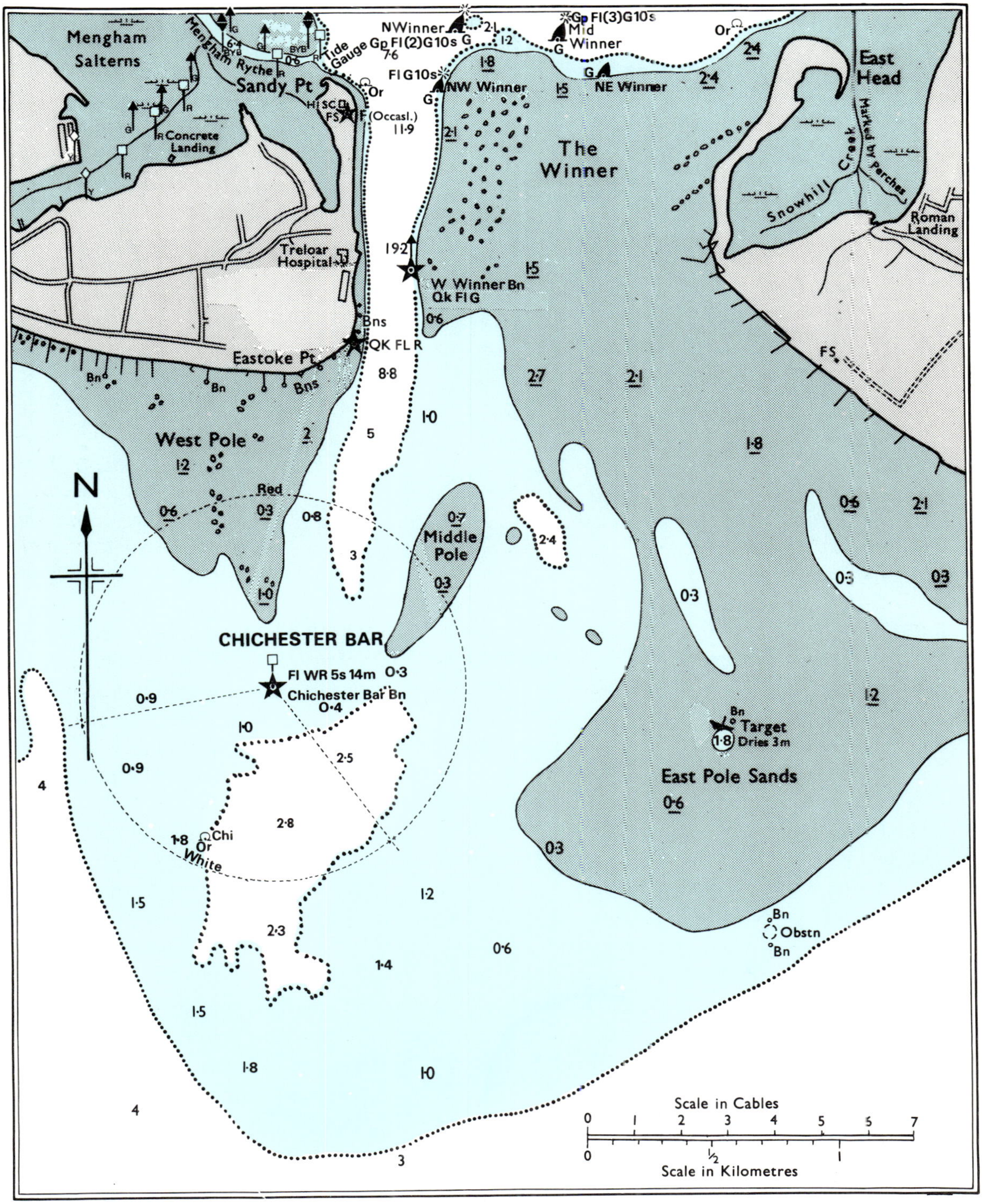

Entrance of Chichester Harbour: Soundings in metres. Add 0·7 m (2·3 ft) at MLWS, 1·8 m (6·0 ft) at MLWN. Based on British Admiralty Chart No. 3418, with the permission of HM Stationery Office and of the Hydrographer of the Navy.

14.1. Chichester bar beacon.

14.2. West Winner Beacon to be left to starboard. Hayling Island Sailing Club can be seen on the west bank of the channel.

this unless she has a commanding wind or auxiliary power. In common with all shoaling lee shores, extra care should be taken if approaching with onshore winds or swell. The approach is dangerous in thick weather and extremely so with strong or southerly gale force winds against an ebb tide.

When approaching from east or west keep well offshore (according to the height of the tide and weather conditions) until the clump of trees at Eastoke Point (see photograph) on the west side of the entrance and Chichester Bar Beacon (*Fl WR 5s 14m*) have been identified, when approach can then be made from due south. Leave the beacon half a cable to port and shape a course to pass midway between Eastoke and West Winner Beacons. On this course a minimum depth of water of 1.4 metres at CD will be found just abreast the Chichester Bar Beacon. Shallow patches exist to the east and west of the approach course. Under low water conditions deep draft vessels approaching from the west and southeast should steer courses to arrive at a point at least one mile south of Chichester Bar Beacon before altering course to the northward. This will avoid the shallow patches of the West and East Pole sands. The Chichester Bar Beacon bears a tide gauge which indicates the depth of water above CD, thus if it reads 1·0 metres there will a depth of 2·4 metres half a cable to the east of it.

When the bar has been crossed, the depths slowly increase to 9 ft (2·7 m) when $\frac{1}{4}$ mile off the entrance and at least a depth of 30 ft (9·0 m) in the entrance.

As the entrance is approached, it will be seen that there are three groynes, with drum-topped beacons on their seaward ends, to be left well to port, as they dry 5 ft (1..5 m) and a fourth which has the Eastoke Beacon (*Qk Fl R*) on it. This beacon should be left $\frac{1}{4}$ to $\frac{1}{2}$ cable

14.3. Eastoke Point and conspicuous trees.

to port and beyond it are three more beacons, all to be left to port as the yacht comes into the entrance.

In the entrance channel itself the deepest water lies in the centre of the channel but there is also plenty of water on the west side as the beach is fairly steep-to. The whole of the area east of the entrance channel is choked by a big shingle bank, the Winner, extending over ½ mile from the eastern shore. As the yacht comes to the entrance, Treloar's Hospital will be prominent on the port side, and the channel lies between the shore and the West Winner Beacon (*Qk Fl G*) which is to be left to starboard. Continuing along the western shore, Hayling Island Sailing Club, standing on Sandy Point at the northern end, will be left to port, and 3 cables NE of it lies the green conical buoy, the NW Winner (*Fl G 10s*).

Lights: There is a *Fl WR 5s 14m* light on the Chichester Bar Beacon. Keep well off shore until in the 120° white sector of this light (visible 14 miles). Approach in the white sector after sufficient rise of tide. The beacon on the groin carries a *Qk Fl R* light, while that on the W Winner Beacon shows *Qk Fl G*. These are followed by the NW Winner buoy showing *Fl G 10s* which is left to starboard, by when Fishery buoy's *Qk Fl (6) + LFl 15s* south cardinal light will be seen.

The Emsworth channel is well lit with NW Pilsey buoy showing *Fl G 5s*: Verner beacon (*Fl R 10s*): Marker beacon (*Gp Fl (2) G 10s*) and the two beacons, NE Hayling (*Gp Fl (2) R 10s*) and Emsworth beacon (*Qk Fl (6) + L Fl 15s*). Up Sweare Deep the Sweare Deep beacon shows *Gp Fl (3) R 10s* and the Northney beacon at the entrance to the Northney Marina channel will show *Gp Fl (4) R 10s*. The marina itself is well lit by

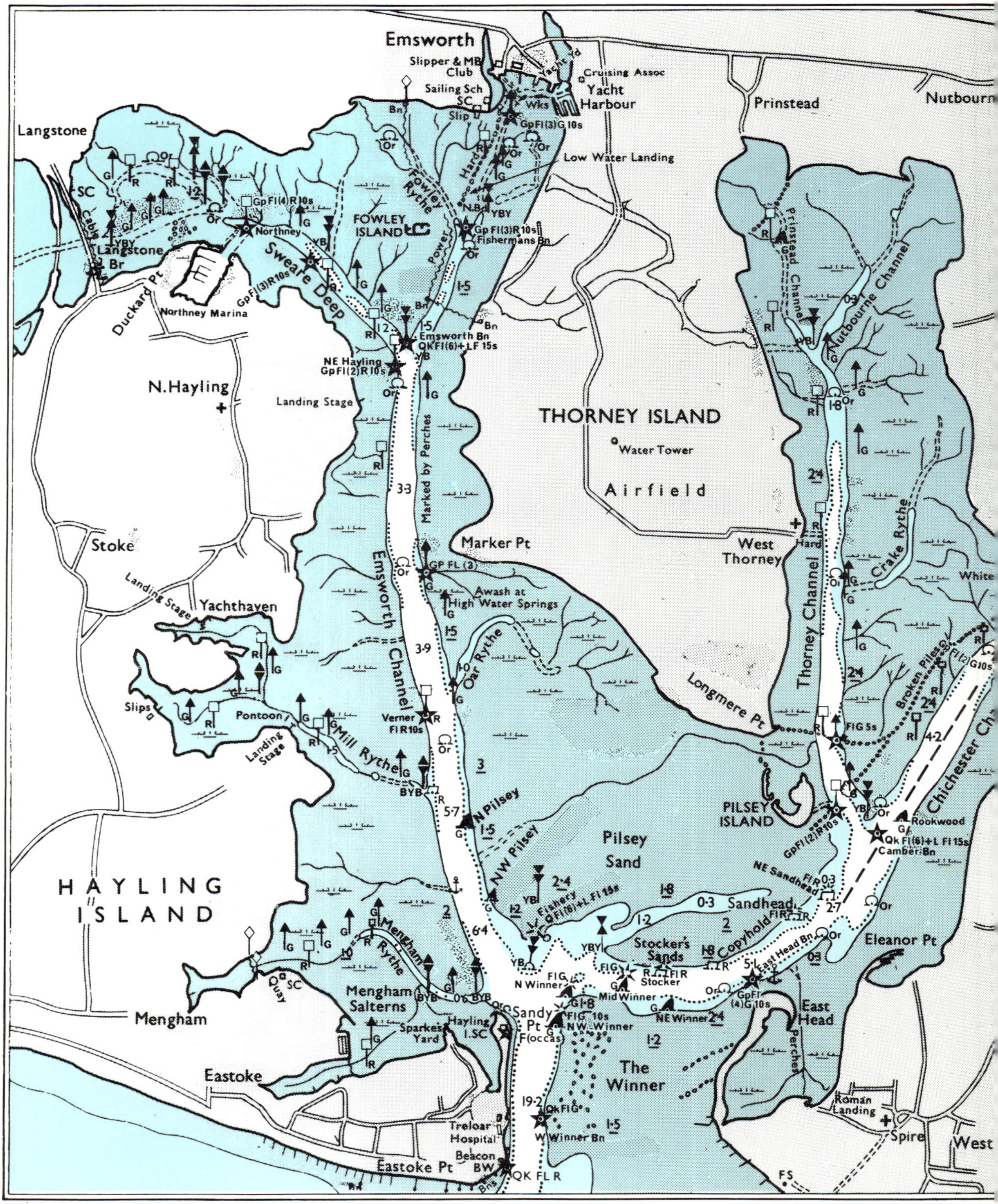

The many channels are liberally marked by perches bearing port, starboard and cardinal top-marks as appropriate. Not all can be shown on this chartlet. The perches and their top-marks have a high casualty rate and one should expect some to be missing.

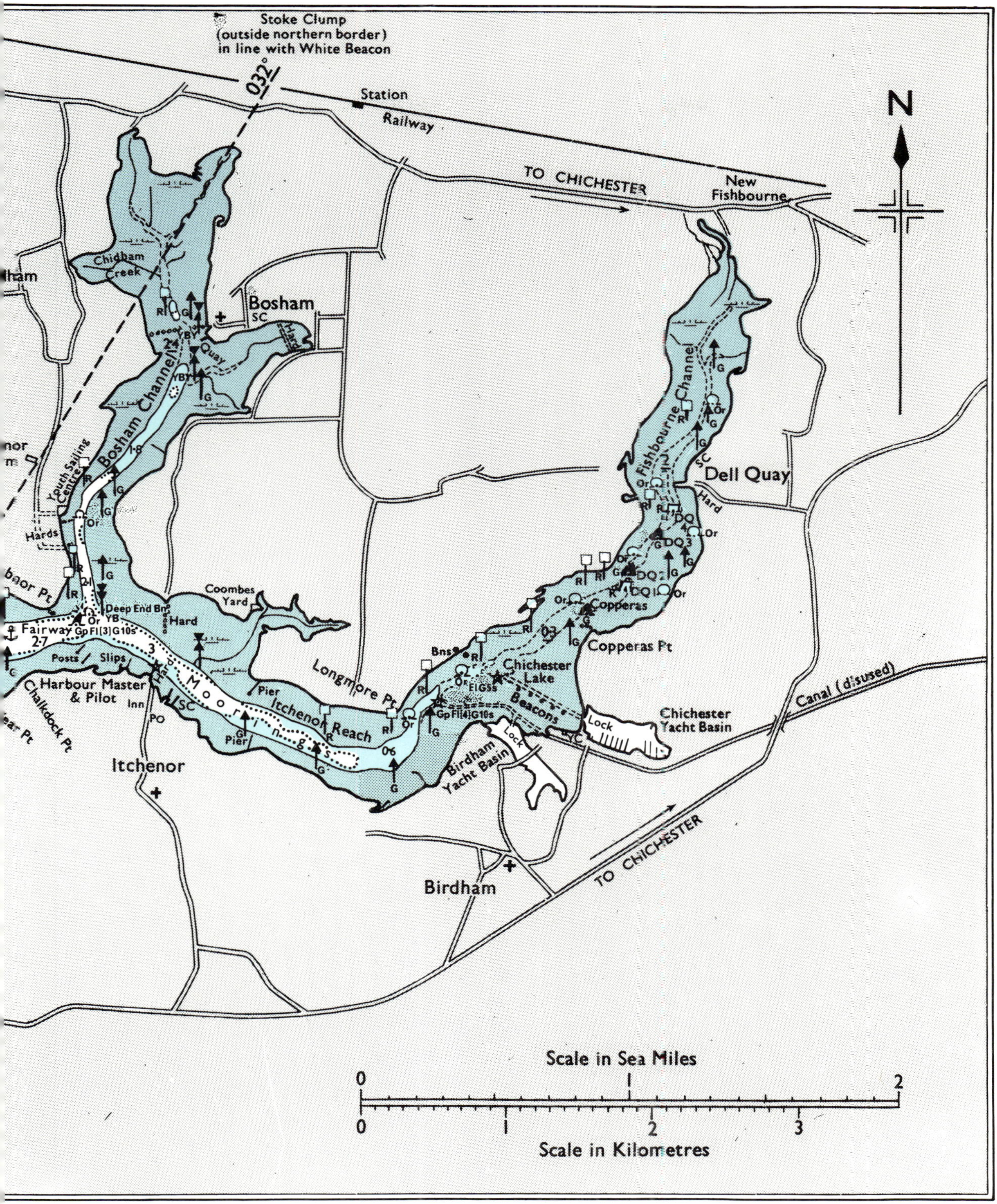
Stoke Clump
(outside northern border)
in line with White Beacon
032°
Station
Railway
TO CHICHESTER
New
Fishbourne
N
Chidham
Creek
Bosham
SC
Quay
Bosham Channel
Youth Sailing Centre
Hards
Deep End Bn
YB
Fairway
Gp Fl(3)G10s
Posts
Slips
Harbour Master
& Pilot
Inn
PO
SC
Chalkdock Pt
Itchenor
Coombes
Yard
Hard
Moorings
Pier
Itchenor Reach
Longmore Pt
Bns
Chichester
Lake
Fl G3s
Gp Fl(4)G10s
Beacons
Birdham
Yacht Basin
Lock
Chichester
Yacht Basin
Canal (disused)
Copperas
Copperas Pt
Fishbourne Channel
SC
Dell Quay
Hard
DQ
Birdham
TO CHICHESTER
Scale in Sea Miles
0
1
2
0
1
2
3
Scale in Kilometres

pontoon lights and will be quite apparent. The northerly channel to Emsworth and the Emsworth Yacht Harbour is lit by Fishermans beacon showing *Gp Fl (3) R 10s* and beyond, Echo beacon with *Gp Fl (3) G 10s.*

The Chichester channel is similarly well lit as far as Itchenor: the N Winner (*Gp Fl (2) G 10s*), Mid Winner (*Gp Fl (3) G 10s*) buoys and the East Head beacon *(Gp Fl (4) G 10s)* mark the starboard side of the channel, while Stocker (*Gp Fl (3) R 10s*), Sandhead (*Gp Fl (4) R 10s*) and NE Sandhead (*Fl R 10s*) buoys mark the port hand and northerly side. From here will be seen the Camber beacon with the south cardinal light *Qk Fl (6) + L Fl 15s* marking the division of the Thorney and Chichester channels.

In the Thorney channel the Pilsey Island beacon (*Gp Fl (2) R 10s*) marks the port side of the gap in the first line of broken piles and a further beacon showing *Fl G 5s* marks the starboard side of the gap in the second line of broken piles.

The Chichester channel continues lit by the Chaldock beacon (*Gp Fl (2) G 10s*) and Fairway buoy (*Gp Fl. (3) G 10s*). The Harbourmaster's pontoon at Itchenor is lit by 2 *FG* (vert). After this there are only the Birdham beacon (*Gp Fl (4) G 10s*) and the CYB beacon (*Fl G 5s*) that mark the channels to the Birdham Yacht Basin and the Chichester Yacht Basin respectively.

THE CHICHESTER CHANNEL

The directions will have brought the yacht within the entrance off Sandy Point and course altered to starboard to pass between the N Winner buoy (starboard) and the Fishery buoy to port. There is something in the nature of an inner bar extending from the N Winner buoy to the west end of the drying part of the Stocker's Sand. The least water is 7 ft (2·1 m) except for a 5 ft (1·5 m) CD patch about ½ cable NE of the N Winner buoy. The course then becomes almost due east and the channel soon deepens. It leads between the Stocker Sand on the north side—steep-to and dries 6 ft (1·8 m) in parts—and the Winner

14.4. Fishery South Cardinal buoy, but without it's top-mark.

14.5 In the distance Stoke Clump is over the middle of the trees and the Roman Transit beacon in transit at 032°.

Sand on the south. The former is marked by the red can Stocker (*Gp Fl (3) R 10s*) and Copyhold port hand buoys and the latter by the Mid-Winner (*Gp Fl (3) G 10s*) and NE Winner starboard hand green conical buoys. After passing between the Copyhold and NE Winner buoys the channel bears to the NE, leaving the sandy promontory of East Head to starboard and the Sandhead red can buoy (*Gp Fl (4) R 10s*) to port.

After passing the latter buoy a very conspicuous distant clump of trees called Stoke Clump will be seen (except in hazy weather) to the NE and in the nearest distance, about 1½ miles away, will be seen a wooded shore. The correct course up the next reach of Chichester Channel is held by keeping Stoke Clump over the middle of the trees on the wooded shore and on with a white rectangular beacon on the foreshore 3 cables west of Cobnor point at 032° (see photograph). If Stoke Clump is obscured there is Roman Transit Beacon in foreground which can be used. It is best to steer on a transit because some of the perches on the starboard hand in this reach are far up on the mud, which extends over ¼ mile from the shore and is covered near high water, creating a hazard on which many yachts run aground. The Transit leads close to the Camber, south cardinal beacon (*Qk Fl (6) + L Fl 15s*) situated on the NE side of the entrance to the Thorney Channel. This should be left to port and, continuing up the main channel, the broken piles and stumps of the old proposed embankment will lie well up on the mud beyond the port hand perches the whole way to Cobnor.

Towards the end of this reach at the Chaldock beacon (*Gp Fl (2) G 10s*) the channel bears to the east and the beacon is rounded leaving it on the starboard hand, as the mud extends nearly 3 cables from the shore with two measured distance beacons with triangle tops high up on it. The channel then runs south of Cobnor Point leaving the Deep End beacon and

14.6. Camber Beacon.

14.7. Roman Transit

the entrance to Bosham Channel to port and passing the green conical Fairway buoy (light now added: *Gp Fl (3) G 10s*) on either side as it is in deep water. South of the buoy is another pair of measured distance beacons, 3040 ft from the first pair. The channel turns about ESE into the Itchenor Reach, and is wide and well marked. This reach leads past Itchenor, a charming village of red-toned houses and cottages on the south side. The fairway is crowded by lines of yachts on moorings but a passage is left between them.

The channel continues for nearly a mile beyond Itchenor before bending round Longmore Point (off which the channel is marked by several red can perches) to a north and then more north-easterly direction. The reach beyond this is not nearly so well marked and can only be navigated with sufficient rise of tide. As far as the entrance to Birdham Pool there is 1 ft (0·3 m) CD, but the mud extends a long way from the southern shore and the best water is on the northern side.

The creek leading to Birdham Pool and Chichester Canal is entered by leaving Birdham Bn (*Gp Fl (4) G 10s*) to port and a series of BW perches to starboard. The dredged channel to the entrance of Chichester Yacht Basin is about 2 cables beyond; it is marked on the starboard hand by six green piles with triangle tops. Do not steer direct from Birdham beacon to the CYB beacon as this course crosses drying mud on the starboard hand. Steer to leave both Birdham and CYB beacons about half a cable to starboard and do not alter course to enter the dredged channel until two leading marks, BW perches with crosses on the shore on the port hand, come into line. Then follow their transit to the CYB beacon and follow the dredged channel.

If continuing up the Chichester Channel to Dell Quay, leave the transit when the CYB beacon is about ½ cable distant and steer for the green buoy off Copperas Point, leaving it to starboard. The channel dries only 1 ft (0·3 m) but is narrow and winding for the first 2 cables NE of the pile, so a stranger may not find the best water. Beyond Copperas Point the channel is shallower, drying about 4 ft (1·2 m) CD, thus having no more than 2 ft (0·6 m) at

14.8. Dell Quay

LW neaps. In the reach between Copperas Point and Dell Quay there are four barrel buoys to mark the narrow winding course. The first and last are red port hand, and the two between are green starboard hand, although when rusty they can be mistaken for red. After passing the last buoy the best water lies towards the end of the quay.

Thorney Channel

In this channel there is 6 ft (1·8 m) and more in most parts to within $\frac{1}{4}$ mile of the junction of the two creeks at its head. The entrance lies to the south-west of the south cardinal Camber beacon, which leave about $\frac{1}{2}$ cable to starboard when entering the channel. The area in the vicinity northward of the buoy has been getting shallower of recent years, so do not try short cuts. An orange racing buoy is often moored near the Camber beacon. On the SE side of Pilsey Island on the port hand is a line of broken piles marked near its end by a red beacon (see photograph) which should be left close to port. On the opposite side of the channel there is the end of the similar line of broken piles to Cobnor, previously referred to. At the end of this is a dangerous shoal which dries out 5 ft (1·5 m) on which there is usually (but not always) a green perch and must be left to starboard. About 3 cables farther up the channel, east of Longmere Point, there are similar lines of broken piles on each side. The narrow fairway between them is marked by an iron beacon with red can top on the port hand side and a green beacon with triangle top to

14.9. (Left) Port hand beacon off Pilsea (Right) Two beacons off Longmere Point marking lines of broken piles on each side of the Thorney Channel.

starboard. From here the channel runs northward and is marked by occasional perches, but note the 4 ft (1·2 m) shoal on the E side off the entrance to Crake Rythe SE of West Thorney.

At West Thorney there is the Thorney Island SC, RAF, and a hard. A number of yachts and small craft lie on moorings in this part of the channel. Thorney Channel divides at its end into two little creeks which run up to Nutbourne and Prinstead villages. Larger vessels should not proceed beyond the junction without local knowledge.

On Thorney Island there is a small village with a church, the sailing club, and a farm, but no shops nor facilities. Most of Thorney Island is RAF property and there is no access by road from the mainland to the hard, club and church, except by permission. There is plenty of room to anchor in Thorney Channel, and shallow draft boats and dinghies can go up on the tide to Prinstead where there is a boatyard, T. H. Payne.

Pilsey Island is uninhabited, and is little more than a semi-circular sea wall. There was once a building upon it, and it used to be a pleasant place for picnics or for parties looking for cockles on the sand flats.

Bosham Channel

One of the most picturesque parts of Chichester Harbour is at Bosham, and the channel is easy to navigate though there are many yachts moored there, leaving a rather narrow fairway. The entrance of the creek runs in a northerly direction out of the main Chichester Channel half a mile west of Itchenor. The south cardinal Deep End beacon (unlit) marks the north east of the entrance, and it is best to keep fairly near this, giving Cobnor point on the port hand a wide berth. The first reach runs north and the channel is clearly marked by the numerous moorings.

The creek is a fathom (1·8 m) deep or over until within about $\frac{1}{4}$ mile from the village, when it shallows and almost dries out a cable from Bosham Quay. Beyond this, Chidam hard, on the west side, extends three-quarters of the way across the creek, and it is mostly submerged at high tide; a post marks its eastern extremity and there is also a hard on the Bosham side. Above the narrows there is a narrow channel but at high water it forms quite a wide lake.

Moorings, Anchorages and Facilities

Chichester Harbour is one of the places in which it is still possible to find room to anchor, but as all parts near the villages and facilities are occupied by moorings, it is best to consider these first. As stated previously, the Harbour Master (Capt Ian Mackay RN (ret'd) controls all the moorings which are rented to yacht owners and for which there is

14.10 Deep End beacon at the entrance to Bosham channel.

usually a waiting list. His office is at Itchenor Hard, facing the river, Tel: Birdham 512301, where there is a Port Operation and Information Service, VHF (FM) Radio telephony. There is a visitor's W buoy (see photograph), off the hard (it is usually vacant as a heavy charge is made for its use after an hour). There are harbour authority moorings in the Itchenor and Bosham Channels and also private moorings which can be used when the owners are away, by arrangement with the Harbour Master, but which on no account should be picked up without enquiry.

14.11. Itchenor hard and the Harbour Master's pontoon. Visitors' mooring in the foreground.

The yacht yards also have a few moorings and enquiry can be made of them on the chance of one being vacant. Alternatively, a berth may be available in one of the marinas which offer all facilities, including yacht yards, chandlery, fuel and stores. It is necessary to wait for sufficient water to reach them.

At **Birdham Pool** there is access to the approach channel about 3 hours either side of HW depending on draft, and the lock gates can be opened 2 hours each side of high water with free flow in the lock for 1 hour at springs. At the **Chichester Yacht Basin**, 2 cables farther on, the river outside dries at CD, but in the channel dredged through the mud to the entrance there is about 3 ft LW on an ordinary spring tide and more at LW neaps. Yachts may secure to the beacon piles or to piles either side of the lock gates while waiting entry. The lock gates to the basin can be opened at any time and there is free flow for 1 hour springs or 4 to 5 hours neaps. Lock control is indicated by boards: red (wait), green (enter) by day; at night the boards are floodlit and only when there is free flow a *Qk Fl* amber light is exhibited on top of the lock tower.

Anchorage, generally speaking, is possible almost anywhere in Chichester Harbour clear of moorings. This restriction rules out the Bosham Channel and Itchenor Reach, but anchorage may be found farther west of the entrance of Bosham Creek between the Fairway buoy and Chaldock beacon. Avoid anchoring near the starting line for races. There is still plenty of room to anchor in the Thorney Channel though it is far from facilities. The anchorage in the main channel, east of the NE Winner buoy off East Head (which is not so steep-to as it used to be) is sheltered in easterly and southerly winds and provides good

14.12. (Left) Verner beacon half way up the Emsworth Channel, and (right) Marker beacon just off Marker Point in the Emsworth Channel.

holding ground and landing on sand dunes, so it is very popular for picnicing and bathing. The West Wittering SC is at the head of the creek (marked by perches) which joins the main channel just east of East Head. Likewise there is anchorage north of Sandy Point at the entrance of Emsworth Channel in westerly winds. Obviously, in the selection of anchorages shoal draft yachts, multi-hullers and twin-keelers have an advantage as they can find room that is not available to deep-keeled yachts in more remote creeks and places where they can dry out at low water.

Facilities. At Itchenor there are excellent facilities as it is the home port of cruising yachts of all kinds and is a notable dinghy and small class racing centre, based on the very active Itchenor SC. Yacht yards include Itchenor Shipyard (also for chandlery and fuel barge), G. Haines and Sons, H. C. Darley and Sons (also chandlery and fuel). E. Bailey, marine engineers, also supply fuel. Launching site at hard. Water at yards or, by permission of club, at their pontoon-jetty. 'Ship' hotel, PO, and general stores (keeps open week-ends in summer). Itchenor EC Thursday. Buses to Chichester.

At the picturesque Dell Quay there is the sailing club, the Dell Quay Yacht Yard Ltd, Wyche Marine Ltd, an inn with restaurant, and 20 minutes walk to shops and garage. It is possible to dry out alongside the end of the quay on hard bottom, but mud on N and S of quay. Public hard north of quay. Moorings for shoal draft craft may be available on application at yacht yards but they all dry out. It may be of interest to add that in the late Roman era the Fishbourne Channel was much deeper and big ships came right up to Fishbourne, a mile west of Chichester. The excavations of the palace of the British vassal king, consisting of a rectangle round a courtyard, reconstructed gardens and quays where the ships tied up, are open to the public.

14.13. Bosham Quay, Sailing Club and church.

Bosham also caters well for yachtsmen. It is possible for a yacht to dry out alongside the quay (by permission of the Quay Master) where there is the Bosham SC. Launching site at quay or street end. Several yacht and boatyards including Burne's Shipyard Ltd, who also supply water, fuel and chandlery, and E. M. Coombes who is in Furzefield Creek, opposite Itchenor. Water at Bosham quay. In the village there are shops and a PO. EC Thursday. Buses to Chichester and Portsmouth.

THE EMSWORTH CHANNEL

The Emsworth Channel is a straight, broad, deep, well marked fairway as far as its junction with Sweare Deep and, with sufficient rise of tide, it continues navigable up to Emsworth, where there is a yacht harbour and excellent facilities. With the aid of the lights referred to below, navigation is now possible at night under suitable conditions.

The channel is entered between Sandy Point and the Fishery buoy (*Qk Fl (6) + L Fl 15s*). A line of yachts on moorings will lie on the port hand and to starboard the green NW Pilsey buoy (*Fl G 5s*). The next mark is the green N Pilsey buoy, followed on the port hand by the red can buoy marking the entrance to Mill Rythe. Three cables north of this and also on the port hand is Verner beacon (*Fl R 10s*). A further six cables takes one to Marker Point and the Marker beacon (*Gp Fl (2) G 10s*).

About ¾ mile beyond Marker Point is the junction where Sweare Deep joins the main channel to Emsworth. Between the two channels lies a large expanse of mud flats intersected by creeks and covered at HW except for the small Fowley Island, which is little more than two disused salterns surmounted by a sea wall.

On the port hand the NE Hayling beacon (*Gp Fl (2) R 10s*) marks the bend to the north west of Sweare Deep. A little further north and marking the middle ground of the junction of the two channels is the south cardinal Emsworth Beacon (*Qk Fl (6) + L Fl 15s*). This prominent beacon is at the end of a line of pile moorings or trots along the west side of the Emsworth channel (see photograph). The Emsworth Beacon also carries a tide gauge

14.14. Emsworth beacon and the line of mooring piles on the starboard side of the Emsworth Channel.

indicating the depth of water over sill at the Yacht Harbour. The fairway is clearly indicated by the moorings. About five cables further up from the Emsworth Beacon is Fishermans Beacon (*Gp Fl (3) R 10s*). This is almost abreast of Fowley Island and marks the junction of three narrow creeks. The one on the port hand is Fowley Rythe and has 4 to 2 ft (1·2 to 0·6 m) CD, for a short distance, in which there are yachts on moorings. The starboard hand creek is Little Deep, and has at least 3 ft for nearly 2 cables on ordinary tides at LW, with moorings for local yachts of light draft.

The principal creek between the two continues up to Emsworth. It becomes narrow and shallow and runs almost parallel to Fishermans' Walk, a long hard over the mud from Emsworth almost to Fowley Rythe which dries about 2 hours either side of LW, and has a notice board at its end. The channel is marked a further five cables on by Echo Beacon (*Gp Fl (3) G 10s*). The wrecks that used to be a feature here have been removed. The creek divides again at Echo Beacon, the port hand creek leading to Emsworth quay and the other

14.15. Fisherman beacon on the middle ground where the Emsworth Channel divides near Fowley Island.

to Emsworth Yacht Harbour. The channel is very narrow but marked by perches. The sill at the entrance is 7 ft (2·1 m) so the depth above it at HW is approximately the Portsmouth height less 7 ft. For example, if the Portsmouth tide table shows a tide of 14 ft 2 in (4·3 m) there will be about 7 ft 2 in (2·2 m) on the sill.

The following are creeks on the west side of the Emsworth Channel in order from the entrance:

Mengham Rythe: The entrance to this creek is north of Sandy Point and has an east cardinal perch with tide gauge placed high on the mud flats on the starboard side. There is a bar at the entrance with only 1 ft (0·3 m) CD but within the creek there are pools with 4 to 8 ft (1·2 to 2·4 m) and even one of 20 ft (6·0 m). The channel is marked by perches but the yachts on moorings in the centre are the best guide to its direction. Less than 3 cables from the entrance there is a junction. The port hand creek dries out and leads to Eastoke and Sparkes boatyard (just west of Sandy Point) with a depth of about 9 ft (2·7 m) at HW but the main channel bears NW and continues to be 6 to 8 ft (1·8 to 2·4 m) deep until it bends to the SW after which it becomes very narrow and soon dries out. The upper reach is navigable by dinghies and craft of shoal draft and leads to Salterns Quay and Mengham Rythe Sailing Club, which has a week-end bar. There is a hard and boatyard and ½ mile distant is Mengham village, with PO, garage and shops.

Mill Rythe: The entrance to this creek lies about ¾ mile north of Mengham Rythe. It is marked on the south side by the red can Mill Rythe buoy which, as mentioned, is a port hand buoy for the main Emsworth Channel, and on the mud on the north side by an east Cardinal perch. The creek is marked by perches, red can tops port, green triangles starboard. For the first ¼ mile the bottom is uneven, and dries out 1 ft (0·3 m) at CD for a cable before deepening and widening with from 1 to 5 ft (0·3 to 1·5 m) as far as the remains of the pier at Wall Corner. It then dries out again and divides into two winding creeks, the northern one leading to Yachthaven and the southern to Hayling Yacht Co Ltd and A. E. Freezer Ltd, which can be reached with sufficient rise of tide. Facilities at yacht yards. PO, shop and bus stop ½ mile inland.

Sweare Deep: This wide channel runs from its junction with the Emsworth Channel in a NW direction between extensive mud banks. It is entered by leaving to port the NE Hayling beacon (*Gp Fl (2) R 10s*). There is often a round orange racing buoy moored near the entrance. Sweare Deep has increased in significance since the opening of the Northney Marina and is clearly marked by the Sweare Deep Beacon (*Gp Fl (3) R 10s*) five cables up on the port hand, and by the Northney beacon (*Gp Fl (4) R 10s*) about three cables on at the entrance to the short dredged channel to the Marina. The channel is also marked by perches (red can to port; green triangle to starboard). There is a least depth of 4 ft (1·2 m) as far as the Sweare Deep Beacon and much of it is 6 to 8 ft (1·8 to 2·4 m). There are oyster beds on the starboard side of the channel with 'keep off' notices. Sweare Deep is well sheltered from SW winds and, although there are many moorings, it provides a good anchorage but rather remote from facilities.

Northney Marina and the channel to it are said to have a least depth of 3½ ft (1·0 m). Berths can usually be found for visiting yachts but there is no water laid on and no provision for fuel. However repairs can be undertaken by Cobra Yachts Ltd and there is a chandlery shop.

Depths decrease as the Northney beacon (*Gp Fl (4) R 10s*) is approached and beyond this the channel divides into three, all of which dry out at CD. There are two east cardinal perches on the middle grounds between the branches of the channel, two going north west, the main one west, and there is also often a round orange racing buoy in the channel between the perches.

The westerly arm leads to Langstone Bridge and thence to Langstone Harbour (see Langstone Channel page 116). When entering this channel leave the east cardinal perch to starboard and the line of small yachts on moorings to port. Once past the entrance to the

14.16. The channel to Langstone Bridge, showing two east cardinal perches (one has had a knock!), that are left to starboard.

channel the rest is easy, as although narrow and shallow it is well marked by perches, Near the bridge is the West Cuts west cardinal beacon to be left to port when proceeding west.

The entrances to the two NW arms are separated by the more easterly of the two east cardinal perches already mentioned. These arms join again about 2 cables on where the middle ground is further marked by a west cardinal perch. The channel then continues in a semi-circular bend to Langstone village and sailing club, and finally south to join the other arm near Langstone Bridge.

At Langstone village there is Langstone Sailing Club and the Ship Inn, with car park and public hard (launching site when room) adjacent at NE end of bridge. The hard on NW is leased to the sailing club. Buses to Havant and Hayling. There is a dinghy hard and park at Duckard Point on the south side of channel ¼ mile east of the bridge, where land reclamation is in progress.

Moorings, Anchorage and Facilities

Emsworth has become an important yacht centre and there is anchorage in the Emsworth Channel and associated creeks anywhere clear of moorings, cables and the fishery areas (marked by notice boards on perches) mostly on the east bank of the channel. The Harbour Master's office is at Itchenor, and the whole of Chichester Harbour, including Emsworth, is centred under his Authority. There are innumerable moorings within the area which are privately rented and application should be made to the harbour master or at the Yacht Harbour to ascertain whether any are temporarily vacant.

There are scrubbing piles at Emsworth, just off the sea wall and at Itchenor beside the hard: apply to the Harbourmaster.

The principal base in the Emsworth Channel is the Emsworth Yacht Harbour. As stated, the approach channel dries out so that it can only be reached with sufficient rise of tide, but it provides 200 berths afloat alongside piers or to pontoons or piles for yachts ranging from 2 ft (0·6 m) to 7 ft (2·1 m) draft. The surroundings are not picturesque, but the facilities are exceptionally good and the charges moderate. Associated with the yacht harbour is a yacht yard, marine engineers, shop with chandlery, brokerage, car park, slipways, fueling jetty and water. There are other yacht yards including T. H. Payne and the successors of J. G. Parham & Sons. John Illingworth and Associates have their yacht designing and brokerage office. Several firms supply chandlery. Launching site at public hard or yacht harbour. Small hotel and Haut Brion restaurant. Emsworth has all other facilities of a small town. EC Wednesday. Station and good bus service.

14.17. Northney beacon (before its light was fitted) and the entrance to Northney Marina.

Appendices

Useful Telephone Numbers

Harbours where no local Custom's Office. Apply Southampton 29251, Cowes 2011 or Portsmouth 20055.

Ashlett Esso SC, Fawley 891440
Creek Master, Fawley 848307
Beaulieu River Harbour Master, Buckler's Hard 200
Yacht Harbour, Buckler's Hard 200
R Southampton YC, Buckler's Hard 213
Bembridge General Manager, Bembridge 2828
Berthing Master, at HW Bembridge 2973
Berthing Master, at LW Bembridge 3635
Cowes Harbour Master, Cowes 3952
HM Customs, Cowes 3132
Cowes Yacht Haven, Cowes 5724
Medina Yacht Harbour, Newport 526733
Island SC, Cowes 6621
Chichester Harbour Master, Birdham 512301
HM Customs, Birdham 512287
Birdham Shipyard (Marina), Birdham 512310
Chichester Yacht Basin, Birdham 512731
Emsworth Yacht Harbour, Emsworth 5211
Bosham Quay Master, Bosham 573336
Bosham Sailing Club, Bosham 572341
Hayling Island Sailing Club, Hayling Island 3768
Itchenor Sailing Club, Birdham 512400
Fareham & Portchester Portchester Sailing Club, Cosham 76375
Fareham Sailing and Motor Boat Club, Fareham 280738
Wicor Marine Ltd, Fareham 237112
Hamble River Harbour Master, Locks Heath 6387
HM Customs, Hamble 2007
Hamble Point Marina, Hamble 2464
Mercury Yacht Harbour, Hamble 2741
Port Hamble Marina, Hamble 2741
Swanwick Yacht Marina, Locks Heath 4261
Royal Southern YC Sec, Hamble 3271
Keyhaven River Warden
Keyhaven YC Sec, Milford-on-Sea 2165
West Solent Boat Builders, Milford-on-Sea 2080
Langstone Harbour Harbour Master, Hayling Island 3419
HM Customs Portsmouth, Portsmouth 20055
Locks Sailing Club, Portsmouth 29833
Tudor Sailing Club, Portsmouth 62002
Eastney Cruising Assoc, Sec, Portsmouth 734103
Lymington Harbour Master, Lymington 72014
HM Customs, Lymington 74584
Lymington Marina, Lymington 75444
Lymington Yacht Haven, Lymington 75999/72853
Royal Lymington Yacht Club Sec, Lymington 72677
Newtown River Berthing Master, Calbourne 429
Portsmouth Harbour Queens Harbour Master, Portsmouth 22351. Ext 22169
Commercial Port Harbour Master, Portsmouth 20436/7
HM Customs, Portsmouth 20055
Camper & Nicholson's Marina, Gosport 80221
Gosport Borough Yacht Harbour, Gosport 83482
Hardway Sailing Club, Gosport 81875
Royal Albert Yacht Club, Portsmouth 25924
Royal Naval Sailing Assoc, Portsmouth 25324
Southampton British Transport Dock Board, Southampton 23844
HM Customs Waterguard, Southampton 29251
Weather Centre, Southampton 28844
Recorded Forecast, Southampton 8091
Tichfield Haven A/Harbour Master, Stubbington 2768
Hill Head SC, Stubbington 4843
Wootton Creek R Victoria YC, Manageress, Wootton Bridge 882325
Yarmouth I.O.W. Harbour Master, Yarmouth 760300
HM Customs, Yarmouth 760406
Royal Solent Yacht Club, Yarmouth 760256

Buoys and Beacons IALA Buoyage System 'A'

The combined Cardinal and Lateral System (Red to Port)

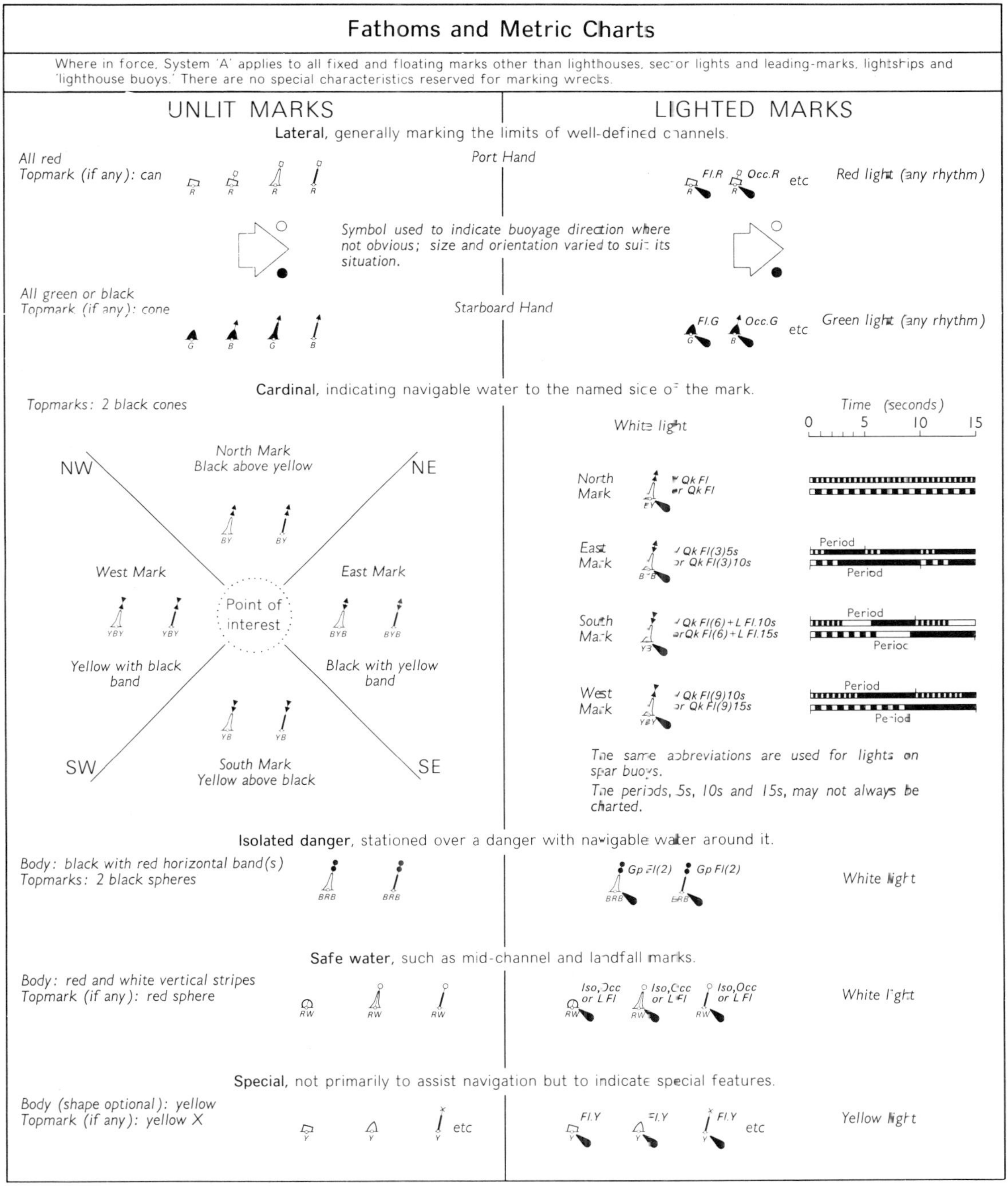

Abbreviated from the book edition of British Admiralty Chart No 5011. With the permission of the Controller of HM Stationery Office and the Hydrographer of the Navy. Stage 3, covering the sea area which includes the harbours in this book is to be implemented during 1979.

Index